# CAPE BRETON ORPHAN

A story of survival, overcoming, and forgiveness

# CAPE BRETON ORPHAN

*a memoir*

RANDALL JAMES

*Authors Note*

This is a true story. However, some names have been changed to protect the innocent.

All dialogue is set off by single quotation marks instead of double, because it is my best recollection of what was said but might not be verbatim.

Text copyright © 2019 Randall James Thompson
Caper Games and Books
All rights reserved.

Published by Caper Books
**www.capergames.ca**

No part of this book may be reproduced, or stored in a retrieval system, or transmitted in any form or by any means, electronic, mechanical, photocopying, recording, or otherwise, without express written permission of the author.

COVER PHOTO:
Sylvia Melanson

COVER DESIGN:
Silke Stein

*I dedicate this book:*

*to my family*

*to orphans everywhere*

*to Capers*

*"I will not leave you as orphans:
I will come to you."*

# 1

## *Launch*

In 1969, Apollo 11 landed on the moon, and in 1969, I met my mother. I was eight years old.

That summer, the Red Barn, a fast-food restaurant in London, Ontario, the town I lived in, held an Apollo 11 contest. You had to collect colourful stickers showing the spacecraft at different points of the mission and sticker them in a large cardboard folder. I vividly remember the photo of the splashdown, the large red-and-white striped parachutes open and the re-entry pod landing in the water.

Customers of the Red Barn received stickers with their purchases, but I think the manager gave me a few each day, even when I didn't buy anything.

I filled all the blank rectangles in the folder over time, and then put it in the draw box. A week later, we received a phone call. I had won! The prize was a meal at the Red Barn for myself, my dad, and my mother. My sister Alison, one and a half years older than I, was able to substitute, which was great, because we didn't have a mother, and nobody wanted to leave out Alison anyway.

# CAPE BRETON ORPHAN

When we went for our free meal, we found out that I had also won a toy: a cool battery-powered robot. It moved around on our table as we enjoyed ourselves and had a great family time.

Which wasn't all that normal because Dad popped in and out of our lives.

He was in the airborne I believe, as I remember photos of him jumping out of aircraft. But that only partly accounts for the shaky existence Alison and I were used to. We moved around a lot, living at different houses and with different people — mostly without our father.

Just like orphans.

I have memories of being with various families through those early years in London. One family took us to a church service. The same people, coming back from a short vacation, gave me a toy western gun and holster set, the belt containing bullets.

Once, there was a flood and we swam in the streets. I distinctly remember this, but sometimes wonder if it was a dream.

Alison and I also lived with the Blairs, an older couple who fixed and sold bicycles. They taught me to ride a bike. We spent the most time with the Blairs out of all the families who looked after us. Their house was close to the Red Barn restaurant.

My dad had a place too, on Dundas Street, a rented room in a building inhabited by people we didn't know, and we stayed there with him when he was in town.

Dad dated various women through the years. One night,

very late, Alison and I woke up from some noise. Dad had a woman over and they were in his bed. We were all sleeping in the one room. I think the woman was French. She made us warm milk, and I drifted off to sleep again after drinking it.

Once, my father showed up after a longer absence with a new full beard, almost unrecognizable, and it scared me.

Two incidents happened during those years that make me wonder today about his mental state.

He had a red VW Bug (with Alison's and my baby shoes dangling from the review mirror). One evening, he took us kids to a drive-in movie with his date. We lay in the back and fell asleep. I awoke during a horror movie and watched a woman in a wedding dress turn into a skeleton. I was so frightened! (It's possible Dad had woken us up to see it.)

Another time, Alison and I were fetched from our beds in the middle of the night and brought down to the basement. My father and his friends had stolen turkeys and were killing them right there and then. The birds ran around in a frenzy, some with their heads cut off. It was loud, bizarre and scary.

Did my dad and his friends do drugs? Sometimes I wonder. I think my dad had grown up as an orphan as well. That would explain a lot.

But Dad did something nice for me once: he saved my life. I was popping PEZ dispenser candies into my mouth, when the spring and plastic top came out and flew into my throat. I was choking.

## CAPE BRETON ORPHAN

There was panic in the house and no one knew what to do. Suddenly, my dad walked in the front door, looked at me and shoved his hand down my throat and pulled the thing out. Wow. It was amazing.

In 1966, Alison and my dad took me to my first day of school. They brought me to the entrance, but I had to go in all by myself.

When I was in second grade, Boyle Memorial Elementary School sent a note to my father, proposing for me to skip Grade 3, but he would not allow it. Looking back, I think it was a good decision.

By that point, we lived close to the Kellogg's (Corn Flakes) plant. Also nearby was Queen's Park. We went there with my father, only a couple of days before my mother came for us. I can remember a few last things with Dad shortly before leaving: having French fries at a restaurant and climbing with him on Engine 86, the old train that stood in the park. Dad knew what was about to happen, but he didn't tell us anything.

One day in the summer, a pretty woman with long dark hair and green eyes showed up at my dad's house.

It was my mother.

She arrived together with a man named Johnny in a black car. I remember meeting her, and going with her to the trunk of the car. She had two new turtle-neck shirts for me: one yellow, the other purple. Both had a large silver ring at the top of the zipper and looked spacey. I put on the yellow one right away.

A short time later, on the same day, my sister and I

sat in the back seat of the black car and drove away with Johnny McPhee and Ma.

So, where had she been all that time?

Years later, I found out. My mother, Deanna, became pregnant at a young age, and was forced to leave her home in New Waterford, Cape Breton, and stay with relatives (the Hubbards) in London, Ontario. There she met my dad, Bob, a friend of the Hubbards. They married shortly after and had three children in quick succession. Bradley was born in January 1959, Alison in December of the same year, and I in May 1961. Ma was nineteen when she gave birth to me.

I have seen a couple of black-and-white photographs of us three kids sitting on the floor together, myself a baby at the time. My mother must have left shortly after, taking only Bradley with her, as she returned to Cape Breton.

Ma told me years later about a train ride from Ontario to Nova Scotia when I was about three. She must have gotten Alison and me for a visit to Cape Breton. While playing in the compartment, I cut my forehead on an ashtray that jutted out from the wall. The accident happened in New Brunswick. They tried to stem the bleeding with a lot of towels, but couldn't, and finally had to stop the train to get medical help. The injury left a small scar at the top of my forehead.

I can't recall any other details of that trip, and I don't know why my mother didn't keep my sister and me then.

But here she finally was, taking us away.

I don't remember saying good-bye to dad, or any tears.

Nothing.

The black car rolled out of his driveway. I felt neither joyful to be with my mother nor sad about leaving my father, or London. I went along with it all. I think I was extremely internal at the time.

The first night of our trip we stayed at a private house in Belleville, Ontario. The owners must have been connected to hockey great Bobby Hull, because they had a signed hockey stick and a big poster of him hanging on the wall. Once in a while, I wonder who it was, because Hull is from the area.

The next day, we got stuck in a major traffic jam in Quebec for a couple of hours. A Quebecois man, the driver of a car in front, brought Johnny a newspaper. It was in French, though, which none of us could understand, but it was still a nice gesture.

We had a long drive, but I don't remember any other particulars.

Did I even know we were on the way to Cape Breton? Did I even understand any of it? I don't think so.

I was on autopilot.

# 2

# *Welcome to Cape Breton*

After two days, we arrived at our new home in Low Point, Cape Breton. When I got out of the car, a boy, a couple of years older than I, came around a barn with sticks in his arms. He had light brown hair and blue eyes, and walked straight towards me.

A few feet away, he stopped, and we just stared at each other in a friendly way. This was my new brother, Bradley. I pulled some French fries out of my pocket and gave them to him. He ate them and smiled. Recently, he told me that they had tasted good.

Low Point would be our new home for the next few years. There was another brother I had not met yet: Junior, four years younger than I and fathered by Johnny.

So, there I was, in a beautiful place — surrounded by trees and green hills. We lived in a little white wooden house with black trim, on a cleared flat spot at the top of White's Lane. Nothing was paved up there. It was all natural ground and grass.

## CAPE BRETON ORPHAN

From that vantage point, you could look down to the blue ocean about half a mile away. To the south were South Bar and Sydney, and to the north, New Victoria and New Waterford. In between the hill and the main highway, which ran very close to the cliffs, were trees, hills, and houses dotted here and there. All around grew blueberries and strawberries.

Behind our house lay Petrie's Lake — and the great thing about this lake was that it froze in the winter and you could play hockey on it!

Only a hundred feet from my new home was another building, covered with black tar paper. It belonged to the MacKays, an older couple. In between our houses was a well, with a square red wooden covering above it.

Our home had three bedrooms. Bradley and I shared one, Alison had another, and the bigger bedroom was for Ma and Johnny. I can't remember which room Junior slept in at this time (maybe in Alison's). There was a small bathroom beside my bedroom, and a small living room with a TV. The kitchen had a coal stove, an off-shoot area for dishes and cupboards, and a pantry with the door that led outside.

As there were now two more mouths to feed, Johnny put in three new vegetable gardens. Bradley and I were responsible for weeding them. We also cut the kindling wood and gathered the coal each day. I remember taking out the garbage to a big dump behind an old wooden outhouse in the woods, nearby the house. A fair-sized snake used to frequent the dump too.

I was glad that I only saw it occasionally.

I made myself a little hiding place in the forest just below our house. I read books there, and I just loved being among the trees. Having my own secret place was important. Looking back, I had psychological issues, and I was wetting the bed at that time.

Ma and Johnny tried to help me. They talked to a doctor, and he recommended various things, like me scrubbing the mattress with soap and water outside the house each time I wet the bed, and also using a plastic sheet under me at night time. A year or two later, I outgrew it — which the doctor told them would happen eventually.

Ma gave me her empty spice bottles and I used them as make-believe medicine for my doctor's office — which was in the out-house.

Low Point was filled with blueberries — big, juicy and so tasty. The ones in the hills just past the MacKays' were the best in the world. In summer time we gathered lots of blueberries for Ma's pies and muffins, but we also put them in empty milk bottles and sold them at the side of the highway — to tourists or locals — whoever stopped. The money went towards school clothes and supplies. Many blueberries didn't make it into our house, though, as I ate lots in the fields. If I took any from a bottle on the side of the road, I would then shake the bottle, so it would appear full again. Bradley showed me that trick.

The summers were endless. Besides berry picking and playing games, we spent lots of time down at the ocean — either climbing the banks or fishing.

## CAPE BRETON ORPHAN

For some reason, I never had a good rod, and my only claim to fame was catching a tiny little perch one year, which I put in my back pocket and brought home to show to everyone. Ma cooked it and I ate it.

There were some excellent fishermen down there and one guy in particular who stood on a rock out in the water. He had a good rod and reel and cast the lure out far. He caught tons of mackerel.

Each winter we would play hockey on Petrie's Lake. I was not a good skater. I don't think I ever skated before, but I loved hockey. This was one big lake. It was the first time I ever heard ice cracking. And if you've never heard it before, it's pretty scary!

You're skating or playing hockey, and you can see the dark under the ice, and then all of a sudden: Crrraaaccck; a long terrifying sound that travels down the length of the lake.

Yet, none of us ever fell in. Well, none of the skaters ...

One winter, at the beginning of the season, Johnny was cutting the ice with his axe to make sure it was thick enough, and somehow Ma, who stood close, crashed through. Fortunately, the water was only up to her waist. It happened right beside the shore, and they managed to get her out without much trouble.

Bradley was a very good skater and hockey player. Being two years older than I, he always seemed stronger and better at everything. Bradley was a Montreal Canadiens fan whereas I loved the Toronto Maple Leafs.

We usually joined in a game of hockey at the lake, and

there were other groups and individuals skating all over the huge ice surface.

During those years, Bradley had a good friend named Brian. His family was very poor, and some local people called them names. It was mean and I never forgot it.

One time, the three of us climbed the banks along the shore, which was a new experience for me. The two older boys were in front and disappeared over the edge, leaving me close to the top. I was stuck and couldn't go up any farther. It was a long way down, and I was pretty scared. I hollered to them, and they quickly re-appeared, laughing. They grabbed my arms and pulled me over. I never felt like they were mean to me, though, just boys being boys.

In the summer, we often went to Austen Robert's store, which was at the end of White's Lane, the winding country road that led from our place to the New Waterford highway. They sold meat and bread and other grocery items, but most importantly, popsicles, ice cream sandwiches and other cold treats. I especially remember the three-coloured Popsicle Pete, and the Buried Treasures drumsticks that had a little plastic figurine hidden under the ice cream.

We got fifty cents each as our weekly allowance, and you could buy a bottle of coke and a bag of chips for less than a quarter.

I entered Grade 3 that first year at my new school, which was aptly named, Low Point School. My classmates had already learned to write the year before, but I had not. My teacher gave me lots of extra attention and turned me into a pretty good writer.

## CAPE BRETON ORPHAN

I loved school. Ma packed us peanut butter and jam sandwiches and some cookies, wrapped in wax paper. I can still smell the inside of the lunch box when opened up.

Ma made me wear a dorky 'Londoner' hat to school in the first year, and some of the boys made fun of me. I slapped one boy and then sat by myself crying. He and some others threatened to beat me up, but thankfully didn't. I wasn't much of a fighter.

Bradley taught me my multiplication tables and always had interesting tricks to show me. For example, how you could do the nine times table by putting down the numbers from 1 to 8 and then writing them backwards on the other side — 8 down to 1. He also taught me that spelling GEOGRAPHY could be remembered as 'George Eaton's Old Goat Ran After Pat Hinchey Yesterday.' I still remember that and chuckle!

One evening, we were studying together in the bedroom. I was lying in bed, close to our table lamp, which had no shade. When I reached for something, my hand accidentally touched the bare light bulb. It left a scar on my hand for many years.

Winnie Chafe was our math teacher. She also happened to be one of the best fiddle players in Cape Breton, and that is saying a lot, because there are many great players there. We did a math test and nobody passed it. She lined up the entire class at the back of the room and proceeded to give us the strap for failing! I remember the parents getting really upset about that.

One day, while we were getting ready for school, Brian

knocked on the door and came in. Bradley was making toast and burned it. He tried to brush off the black crumbs and even put some water on it. The piece of toast was completely ruined, but Brian still wanted to eat it, and did. I felt really bad for him.

Johnny was a very good provider. He worked hard at the Steel Plant in Whitney Pier, and we four children lacked for nothing. He used to take some of the vegetables we grew, put them in the trunk of the Impala and bring them to some black families in the Pier — close to the coke ovens. I was in the car at least one time to see that.

One thing I disliked about Johnny, though, was that he had something against Bradley. He often called him by a nick-name Bradley didn't like.

We owned a family dog, Spotty, white with black spots, part Labrador and part Dalmatian. He was an outside dog and always around. I considered him my dog. Spotty and I were very close. I used to show him my hockey cards, both of us sitting up against the MacKay house.

Another thing I used to do with my hockey cards was making little table-top games at the kitchen table. I cut out the players to make two teams, and crumpled the silver foil from Ma's cigarette package into a ball, which I passed between the players. I also created small baseball games outside in the dirt with sticks and pebbles.

One day, when I was playing road hockey by myself on the field between the houses, Spotty came down from the woods, acting strange. I had a funny feeling about the situation, so I called to him from the other side of the well.

## CAPE BRETON ORPHAN

Sure enough, he walked right into it. Spotty was blind! I hollered towards the house. Ma and Johnny came out and examined him. They discovered that someone had shot him with buckshot right in the face. There were hunters in the area up by Petrie's Lake.

That night, I slept with Spotty on the pantry floor.

Either the next day or shortly thereafter, Alison went to get the newspaper. Back then, you had to walk the long gravel road to the highway, then cross to the other side to pick up the paper that was thrown there. Spotty followed Alison and got hit by a car and was killed instantly. Sometimes I wonder if they just told me that story, but put Spotty out of his misery.

Of course, I was heartbroken, but I still had the woods, the blueberries, the lake and the ocean.

I loved the spectacular beauty of Cape Breton, but I would soon learn that there was another side to the island — a dark side.

# 3

## *Dark Clouds*

My mother was friends with two families in the neighbourhood: the Camerons, who lived close to the main highway, and the Campbells, whose house was about a mile to the north on Campbell's Lane.

Ma used to go for tea to Jeanette Campbell's, and I became close friends with her son Danny, who was my age. Alison befriended his sisters, Teresa, Nora and Karen.

The Campbells owned a big house, large barn and a good-sized property. This was country living at its finest. We went over to their place every once in a while, especially in the winter. They had a pond, and some great hockey games were played there.

One winter, during a hockey game on the pond, Danny's older brother, Colin, whacked me in the left eye with his stick. Blood covered my eye. I had to go to the doctor's and get a patch.

For some strange reason, I had a series of mishaps with my left eye while I lived in Low Point.

## CAPE BRETON ORPHAN

Once in a while, the Campbells came to our place too, especially to play baseball. We had crazy things for the bases, with first base being a big telephone pole! I actually crashed into that one time, with — you got it — my left eye. I must have stumbled as I reached first. Second base was a rock and third was the well. We pitched towards the ocean and hit towards the lake.

For grade five, I had to take a bus to my new school in New Victoria. I played some road hockey there, which was really like field hockey — contested on the bumpy ground in behind the school. Once, I dove in front of a shot, and got smacked in my left eye again! I stood in line to go back in when the bell rang — my eye-lid hanging down. Some of the kids stared at me. The Vice-Principal noticed and took me to his office to put a couple of stitches in. He was a very nice man.

Close to the school was a small store where we used to buy our hockey cards, the packs with the stick of bubble gum in powder. This one year, the cards all had loud colours and bright spotlights in the background. I remember them vividly. My goal was to collect all the Toronto Maple Leaf players. Trading was a big deal then and so was studying all the statistics of your favourite players on the back of the cards.

One day, after school, as I was walking around waiting for the bus, Joey hollered to me, 'Watch out, Randy'. I heard loud running footsteps behind me and ducked. Roy flew over top of me and onto the ground! I had no idea why he attacked me.

All the kids gathered around and moved us towards the side of the school. Roy and I were holding each other by the collars when my hand slipped and punched him in the face. His nose started to bleed and he ran towards home! Problem was, he lived in Low Point. However, it turned out, his dad was driving to the school to pick him up. So, a few minutes later we were both in the Principal's office, getting the strap.

Back in Low Point, things were deteriorating between Ma and Johnny, who favoured Junior over the other kids. One night, Johnny scooped some ice cream for only himself and Junior at the kitchen table while the rest of us sat in the living room. We all knew and this made Ma angry.

In hindsight, there seemed to be some jealousy playing out, as Ma also had a favourite — Bradley.

So, where did that leave Alison and me?

I think the real reason that Ma brought Alison and me to Cape Breton, was because Ma's father, my grandfather, Albert LeDrew, was dying of cancer in the New Waterford hospital. I'm guessing that he and my grandmother, Eva, forced her to come and get us.

Shortly after we landed in Cape Breton, Alison and I visited our grandfather. Some days later, Ma got the phone call in Low Point, and just sat down and cried. As a side note, for a timid eight-year-old boy who just met his grandfather for the very first time, it was bizarre and scary to see him a few days later in an open coffin with all the smells that accompanied that event.

Ma told us later that during her father's final days in the hospital, he heard *Amazing Grace* playing over and over and thought it was on the radio. But it wasn't.

## *The Great Escape*

Despite the growing tension at home, Junior and I got along very well. He was a handsome boy with brown hair and eyes. At the time, he had some kittens whom he loved. He also had an interesting hobby of catching small grass snakes and nailing them to the barn wall. Junior was obviously in a tough situation here, between his father and mother.

Ma claimed that the few times she drove Johnny to work to keep the car for all of us, that the next day he would check the odometer and ask her where she had gone and what she had done. There was a big age difference between them and Ma was not ready to totally settle down — as we shall see.

Ma and Johnny almost never went out drinking and dancing, but now, suddenly they did. Late one night, after they returned home, we were awoken by a loud argument. We all ran into the hallway where we could see into the kitchen. Ma was on the ground and Johnny was crouched over her, holding a beer bottle and threatening to hit her. Alison bravely yelled at Johnny to leave Ma alone. Johnny hollered at Alison and took a step towards her, but Ma shrieked at him. Thankfully, Johnny stopped. He either went to bed or outside for a bit. That was the end of violent things for that night.

## Dark Clouds

Years later, I would see Ma get mouthy when she got drunk (which was far too often), so sometimes I wonder if she was like that during the couple of times her and Johnny went out. (Not that it excuses Johnny's violence).

Another time, we escaped the house at night and had to hide from Johnny. We tried to make it to the Campbells. We walked through the woods about twenty or thirty feet from the road. When we saw car lights we would lay low or freeze and become part of the trees. Once the car was past, we moved again. I guess Ma and Johnny had another falling out, and things were getting worse. I can't remember if we stayed at the Campbells that night, but I'm guessing we did. Ma and Johnny would patch things up again though.

I was troubled in these situations because I really liked Johnny and he always treated me well. I think it was because I was closer to Junior and played with him more than the other kids.

Eventually, Ma made a secret plan with the Camerons, and one day, while I was out in the yard playing hockey, Ma and all the kids came out of the house and briskly walked past me — heading down the road. She signalled for me to join them. I threw my hockey stick on the ground and followed them down White's Lane to the Camerons. I would soon find out we were leaving Johnny for good and moving to New Waterford.

Unknown to any of us kids at the time, we were headed from the frying pan into the fire.

# 4

## *Welcome to New Waterford*

Well, so much for Low Point and New Victoria, we were now off to New Waterford. This meant a new town, school and friends. Not great for a kid who was already pretty shy.

New Waterford was Ma's town, the town of her parents and siblings: Gerry, Florence, Whitney and Beverley. Ma was the middle child.

New Waterford was a coal mining town with a population of around ten thousand, bordered by the ocean on one side and Scotchtown towards the other — divided in the middle by the main street, Plummer Avenue.

The town had a new high school, BEC (Breton Education Centre), which was close to Scotchtown. We thought of the town as 'down' by the ocean or 'up' by BEC, as the roads sloped down, from Plummer Avenue to the ocean.

New Waterford was basically flat and wind-swept with few trees.

## CAPE BRETON ORPHAN

The stores on Plummer Avenue had no real facades, and gave a ghost-town or old-west type feel.

The first house we lived in was a small brown two-bedroom house on Mahon Street, very close to Woolworth's Department store on Plummer Avenue.

My new elementary school was Central, close to the ocean on Hudson Street. I was in grade six. The kids at school were generally nice, especially the girls. There were a couple of tough boys amongst the lads, and I learned quickly that New Waterford was a rough town, where fighting was common. That would be a big problem for such a scared kid as me. I was doing okay in my own internal world, but fisticuffs were not for me.

Actually, that's not entirely true … Remember the ads in the old comic books, where you could order something to make you stronger, like Charles Atlas? (The artwork showed tough guys kicking sand on a weakling). Well, there was an ad to teach a person Karate. So, I ordered it. Ma must have given me the money. I think it was fifty cents.

The package came in the mail one day. It was a cheap booklet with some text and graphics about how to do Karate. So, one day I got into a fight in our back yard with a boy named Patrick. I tried to use a punching technique that I learned from the 'course'. It sort of worked and the fight was pretty even. I remember Patrick rubbing his jaw when it ended. I felt good about it. I guess I had the home field advantage.

I had also discovered a group of boys a few streets down

from our house, who played road hockey and they allowed me to join them for some games. Patrick was one of the players. One of the older guys was named 'Boots,' a pretty intimidating name. I wondered how he got that name.

A great thing happened during grade six at Central. I became friends with Sheldon and his family were into harness racing. They owned a couple of horses and I got to go with them a few times. I loved the track in Sydney and even learned how to place two-dollar bets. I always bet 'show' so that my horse could come in the first three places and I could win some money. This was a very safe bet. I would normally win ten cents or a quarter, and a bit more if my horse actually won. I loved statistics and reading the programs and trying to figure out if my horse could win, or at least place third.

That year, Sheldon's family had an incredible horse: Crescent Tornado — and this horse started to win every race and set records.

On the big 'blanket night' he won his race and got a great new blanket. It was always so exciting to hear the announcer as the horses came down the stretch: 'And here comes Crescent Tornado!'

It wasn't all great with Sheldon, though, because one time at school, during an argument about a line up in gym, he punched me in the gut. I learned what being winded was — because I felt like I was going to die. I couldn't catch my breath. I don't know why he did it. Sometimes I think that boys learn things from their brothers or others and just try them out.

# CAPE BRETON ORPHAN

Some other boys in town introduced me to another New Waterford pastime — stealing! And, because we were poor and didn't have many treats (like chips, pop, and pastries), it didn't take much coaxing to get me on board.

One of the first things I was taught, by a kid named Glen, was how to steal at Woolworths. We would walk in with boots on and roam around until we found something. Our routine was to bend over and shove the items into our boots and pull the pant leg over it. When we did this with chips, we had to walk quietly. This was my apprenticeship, and I would end up stealing lots over the years.

While we lived on Mahon Street, Ma helped me to get a newspaper route with the *Cape Breton Post*. One month, after I collected all the money, I kept it and went on a feast of pies and Jos Louis pastries. I also bought treats for everyone in our house. Ma asked me where I got the money from and I told her it was my profits from the paper route, but she had to know.

Eventually, the *Post* man came looking for the money, and that was it for the route. The worse thing is, looking back, was that I was never taught anything. It's not like Ma scolded me or taught me right from wrong. I got the impression that stealing was okay.

Ma dated a couple of men during this time and one of them was Greg Lafferty. It didn't take us kids long to figure out that he was a complete psycho.

One time, Greg knocked on the back door while Ma was out on a date, and I let him in. He wanted to come into my bedroom and hide in the closet while I asked Ma how her date went. So, when Ma came home, I met her in the kitchen, just outside the bedroom where Greg was hiding. I secretly pointed towards my bedroom, and asked her how her date went. She described it as not-so-great. Good thing. Greg came out and surprised her, and all was well ... for now.

Another night, Greg and his buddy, Dirk, came over to our house and they drank at the kitchen table with Ma — right beside my bedroom and the door was open. Us kids were trying to sleep. Greg threw a glass that smashed close to my head. The adults jumped up and were all apologetic and picked up the shards that were scattered on the bed.

Looking back, I have to wonder why Ma continued to date this guy.

Ma and Greg must have broken up around this time, because he wasn't allowed to come over anymore. One night, while Ma was out, he knocked at the back door, but we didn't let him in. He tried to get his hand through the little open window and unlock the door, but Alison took a fork and stabbed at him. He finally left.

During Ma's new party life, she fell asleep in bed with a cigarette (and it wouldn't be the last time). Us kids woke up in the early morning to a smoke-filled house. We wet cloths and breathed through them as the smoke became thicker and thicker. I don't know why we just didn't go outside. We tried to wake Ma up a couple of times to no avail and finally left the house. Someone called the fire department.

Thankfully, no one was injured, besides smoke inhalation. You have to wonder why child protection never investigated.

Ma and Greg continued their hot and cold relationship, and we soon learned that there would be a new addition to the family. Dennis was born in January, 1975.

Later that year, my family moved to the Low Rentals. This was a housing project for the less fortunate of the town. The buildings were cookie-cutter duplexes with white siding, and had different colours at the top of each one — blue or yellow. The Low Rentals were just past Central Elementary School on each side of Hudson Street, very close to the ocean.

Of course, Greg moved in too. He would terrorize us for a couple of more years. He and Ma got married at some point, however they continued the madness of on again, off again.

One year, at Christmas, one of the kids got a tape recorder with a microphone. It was more like a toy. We all took turns recording something fun on the machine. When it was Greg's turn, he took it into the bedroom and was gone for a long time.

When he returned, he played it for us. 'They're coming to take me away, he he ha ha ho ho. They're coming to take me away he he ha ha ho ho,' he sang over and over and over as he laughed and cried hysterically on the tape. It was chilling and very, very scary. We were all afraid and knowingly glanced at each other, hoping that Greg didn't notice.

One time, Ma went in to get her tubes tied and Greg showed up at our house and stole Dennis while Alison was watching him. I remember Ma arriving in a taxi and freaking out. Dennis was soon returned, but it was just another example of Greg the psycho terrorizing everyone.

In '76, Greg came to the house for some reason. He wasn't living with us anymore, and I don't know if Ma had agreed for him to come over. Ma, Greg and Bradley sat at the kitchen table discussing something. Bradley and Greg suddenly stood up, as they grabbed each others' hands, kind of like wrestling. Bradley was holding his own.

'Help me, Randy,' he said. And I wish I could go back to that moment and punch the crap out of Greg. Instead, I ran outside and hollered for Billie-Joe Drake, our next-door neighbour, to help us.

Billie-Joe came out and hollered, 'What are you doing in there, Greg?'

That's all it took. Another man to stand up to him, and Greg Lafferty ran away, like the little coward he was.

# 5

## *The Hudson Street Years*

We lived in #288, right beside the Drakes. Jackie (aka Jake), the oldest son, became one of my best friends. His parents were the handsome, Billy-Joe and Anna. They had a famous Christmas tree, white with big red balls, displayed in their living room window each year.

There were tons of kids in the neighbourhood, and I quickly made some new friends who all had a great love for hockey! We played road hockey from morning to evening, whenever we could. My friends included: Robbie Loveys (and his brothers, Melvin, Billy and Winston), Jake Drake (and his brothers Billy and Tushie and sister Shannon), Timmy Head, Fred Head, Kevin Head, Jim Burns, Louie Piovesan, Leo Getto (and his brothers, Bradley and Dana) — and Martin Malik, one of my close friends from another hood, but he didn't play a lot of sports with us.

Jake's other sister was Joanna, who seemed to be forever doing dishes at the kitchen window when I hopped the fence between our back yards.

## CAPE BRETON ORPHAN

We would always greet each other: 'Hi Randy.' 'Hi Joanna.'

Some other girls in the area were Linda Drake, Maxine MacKenzie, Missy Syms, Donna Head, and the Loveys girls (Sharon, Valerie, and Brenda).

Our two road hockey nets were kind of famous also. Billy Loveys built a fantastic net from heavy wood and lobster netting! It was so heavy to carry from his house to the Central school parking lot, that sometimes two of us had to carry it. Billy was pretty innovative when I think about it. He mostly played goalie and made sliding knee pads to go over his goalie pads. These plastic white sheets were made from old bleach jugs. This way his goalie pads didn't get wrecked on the asphalt.

Kevin Head had the other net — a normal store-bought light metal net with white netting. During some games, Kevin would get upset about something, like criticism for letting in a bad goal, and threaten to leave and take his net home, just across the street. We'd beg him to stay. It was comical (but not at the time). We desperately wanted to have two nets! Sometimes he would carry out on his threat and we'd then get mad at him.

We also played football in the big open field across from Central and played tons of baseball and football on the field in behind the school. Occasionally, baseballs would end up on the roof of Central and some of the daring boys would climb up and get the balls. They had to climb up two levels to the gym roof, before jumping down to the lower roof to retrieve the balls.

I finally got brave enough to go up there in the later years. It was scary to hang off the gym roof and jump down to the lower part when coming back down.

Sanjiv Maindiratta, who lived on the street at the back of the school, sometimes joined us for hockey, baseball and football, but he often stayed inside and studied for school.

The Maindirattas were a lovely family that came from India and Sanjiv's father was a science teacher. I used to stop and wait for Sanjiv on the way to BEC.

I remember two distinct things about their small green older house: the aroma of Indian cooking, and the tilted floor. This was a hard-working family, in terms of studying. Sanjiv ended up being class valedictorian in '79 when we graduated. His sisters were also amazing with fantastic smiles (Anita, Renu and Rajani).

This brings me to Martin Schwartz, the Honours Chemistry teacher at BEC, who had also immigrated from India. He was brilliant and won a national award one year for teaching. All the brainiacs took his class. He was very nice to me and let me take his class each year.

I felt like I was out of my league in his class and didn't really understand the formulas, but we were always in pairs, and I got teamed up with students like Bernie Matlock or another brain and they carried me. The other students at BEC were getting bad marks in the regular chemistry class, so I was extremely happy when Mr. Schwartz would approve us all each year, to take his class for the next grade.

In 2014, I got the chance to visit Mr. Schwartz a couple of years before he passed away.

I was surprised to find out he was attending Calvin United Church and singing in the choir; the same church we had gone to a couple of times as children.

The one place where I felt equal to the brainiacs was in the chess club. I really got into chess for a couple of years and won the trophy in Grade 12.

I used to walk back and forth to BEC twice a day, coming home for lunch each day. Four trips in total, about two kilometres each way. No wonder I was so skinny! And every noon hour Ma and I played the TV game show *Definition*, which was similar to the word game Hang Man. We were so competitive — always racing to see who could solve the puzzle first. I would then have to hustle to make it back to school on time.

We also competed at *Wheel of Fortune* at night. I started to get them quicker than she as I got older, but it was close. She always wanted me to get on the show.

Ma loved games. In Low Point, Ma and I played a long series of Scat card games (also called 31) into the night. I played for money to buy a new pair of sneakers. I won the last game and won the pot of about two dollars in dimes and nickels. When I won the last game, Ma claimed that she was so bleary-eyed she couldn't really see her cards anymore.

Another interesting thing that happened in Low Point surrounded a toy called Devil's Dice (if I remember the name correctly).

This was a bunch of plastic cubes in a row with various colours on each side. They had to be in perfect order and have different colours on each side and the ends to solve the game. It was kind of like a precursor to the Rubik's Cube — but linear.

Ma and the family went to visit in New Waterford and I asked to stay home and keep working on the puzzle. By the time they returned I had solved it. Ma suggested that I had read the instructions, but immediately reached into her coat pocket and pulled them out. She had a very surprised look on her face realizing that she'd taken them with her!

## *A Creative Soul*

Ma was also a poet. She told me that one of her poems had been selected and read on the radio for Canada's Centennial in 1967.

This is part of it:
*With bannock and molasses what more can ye ask us*
   *It's Canada's birthday on Cape Breton's shore.*

I always thought it was brilliant. That part of the poem is embedded in my mind.

Ma also made her own clothes — buying those patterns to cut and sew everything together. She also baked fantastic bread, pies and tea biscuits.

For all of Ma's faults, she had a wonderful side too.

## *Back to Hudson Street*

Once I became a teenager, I began to babysit. This was a great way to earn extra income.

I babysat for my uncle Whitney and my aunt Beverley. I also babysat for my mom's friend, Dot, and sometimes for families in the neighbourhood.

I also took over Robbie's paper route for the *Cape Breton Post*. This time, I was faithful and did a good job. Once a month, I received a big stack of flyers to deliver, which was a pain, as each one had to be inserted into each paper. To get around this extra chore, Robbie showed me how to build a nice bon fire from a pile of flyers — in the gulley between the Low Rentals and the other side of New Waterford. Problem was, while we enjoyed the fire, we looked up to the road and there stood the Post rep staring down at us. Fired again!

Through the years on Hudson Street, things got worse with Ma's drinking and going out to the bars. She also took Valium for her nerves. On some weekend nights, she would come home with her friends and they would drink till the early hours of the morning. Once in a while, the smell of pot wafted upstairs. When everyone had left and Ma was in a drunken stupor, she would sometimes smash dishes — one time destroying the beautiful small china cabinet that she had refurbished herself. I was the one who had to clean up when Ma finally went to bed.

I know the sickening smell of spilled beer and dirty ashtrays well.

# 6

## *Hudson Street Violence*

Major changes were happening to our family. Alison ran away back to London in '75. She didn't get along with Ma and complained about the many chores she had to do. Bradley joined the Navy in '76. He was only seventeen, so Ma had to give written permission. The plan was for Bradley to send money to Ma each month.

Junior and I stayed close, but he spent more and more time with his father. Being suddenly left as the oldest child remaining at home, I became the de facto babysitter for Dennis, fourteen years younger than I.

### *New Waterford Pirates*

Because of our poverty, I kept stealing through the years. My new friends stole a lot too. Our favourite target was the new Co-op grocery store on Plummer Avenue. We had a system to hand big bottles of pop, bags of chips and peanuts to each other in the store — so that no one could figure out what we were up to.

One of us would pick an item off the shelf and hand it to another. It was passed from hand to hand, until someone took it out of the store. This was repeated until we had what we wanted.

After the raid, we met up at the side of Calvin United Church and shared the spoils in the shadows, wolfing down the peanuts, chips and pop — like a bunch of pirates. I thought about that scene through the years and wondered what God thought about it. Was he mad at us, or were we somehow in his loving protection?

We also stole from the House of Plenty store, up by the baseball diamonds. We called it the House of *Nothing* as we lifted so many pastries and treats there. I feel very bad about that today, as I wonder how much it hurt the family who owned the store.

Hinchey's store was another victim ... and our downfall. We took my brother Junior with us and he made too much noise stealing a bag of chips. *Busted!* The owner hollered at Junior as he ran out the door, but he kept going. Eventually, Ma and the other parents found out and we were all grounded. It was hard for the adults to scold us too much though, as they were thieves themselves.

One evening, I babysat Dennis at home, and somebody knocked at the front door around midnight. I came downstairs and looked out the small front door window. I saw Rosy, Ma's best friend, and another woman standing beside her.

To my horror, it was Ma! At first, I didn't recognize her. I opened the door and let them in.

Greg Lafferty had punched her out on the dance floor at the club. Ma had a black eye, a busted nose and swollen lips.

Over the next couple of days, I waited at the back of our house with a hunting knife in my hand. My friend Robbie stood with me. My plan was to stab Greg, but he never showed up.

In 1978 and '79, Ma dated two brothers. First, she saw Hank, and later, his younger brother, Donnie. They were nice enough guys, but drunks. One night, after coming from the club, the three of them were sitting on the concrete steps outside the front door. It was around one in the morning. A stocky, but overweight guy and his girlfriend walked down Hudson Street, and he hollered something to Hank, Ma's boyfriend. Alerted by the noise, I rushed to Ma's bedroom window, which faced the street.

Whatever was said, Hank bolted to the offender. Hank put his hands up to fight, in kind of an old-fashioned way, but the guy decked him with a thunderous overhand punch. Hank had no chance. He fell to the ground, groaning. The guy started to kick Hank in the face. The sound was sickening. People ran onto the street from all the houses, including Ma, yelling for the guy to stop. Donnie got there first, and the guy flattened him in the same way. Thankfully, he didn't kick Donnie.

I found my pellet gun, loaded it and leaned out the window, the barrel pointed at the head of the bad guy. I knew the gun was not very powerful, but thought I might be able to hit him in the eye.

However, I glanced to my left and spotted Anna Drake leaning out her window.

I changed my mind and withdrew the weapon.

An ambulance was called, and that was the end of another eventful night on Hudson Street.

# 7

## *Graduation*

During my last few years on Hudson Street, I started to drink and smoke. At fifteen I was allowed to smoke in the house, but I was expected to buy my own. I used to roll my own cigarettes, and later used those little hand machines with tubes and tobacco. That's why I needed the extra money from babysitting, the paper route, and other odd jobs.

My friend Martin was a year older than the rest of us and already had a moustache. He also wore a fedora, which gave him a daring look. He helped us buy our first real alcohol — a pint of Lemon Gin. He got an older acquaintance to purchase it.

I got pretty drunk after a few swigs of that! It was during the day time, in the basement of an old abandoned house. Later, we walked around the neighbourhood and I felt way too good. In fact, I told Joanna that I loved her when I ran into her. She chuckled and said, 'Tell me that when you're sober, Randy'. I never did.

## CAPE BRETON ORPHAN

Over the next few years, my friends (mainly Robbie, Jake, Timmy, Leo & Martin) and I drank more and more, and started to go to the dances in New Waterford — where fights occurred often.

One night, Timmy and I went to a dance at the New Waterford rink. Normally, the girls and their partners danced in the middle, and the guys walked around them in a large circle. The rest of the crowd milled about.

Timmy and I had just arrived and started to walk in the circle. *Bam!* I saw stars! I was sucker punched in the throat. Timmy took off (I don't blame him). I walked a few more feet and then stopped, holding my throat. I looked back and a big gang walked up to me. I waited in fear.

Soon, a stocky guy and his girlfriend, leading the pack, came up to me and he grabbed me by my shirt – glaring at me. 'That's not the guy,' he finally said to his girlfriend, and let me go. He was drunk. Man, was I happy to get out of there. I went home and had a sore throat for days.

By age sixteen, I was six foot three and very skinny. When outsiders came to our neighbourhood to play sports, I was a target. I just didn't fight, and they knew it. I saw myself as kind of a Borje Salming or Mike Bossy — NHL players who didn't like to mix it up.

One time, a guy from another part of town — who only played road hockey with us once, pretended that he was going to punch me out, so I turtled. Everyone laughed, but nothing happened. I popped back up and we just kept playing.

Another time, at the back of the school, another new

kid started throwing punches at me. I blocked all of them. He finally got frustrated and just gave up. I think that if I had a good dad in my life, he might have said, 'Son, if you can block all those punches, you can probably throw a couple too.'

## *My Big Fight*

However, there was one time that I did fight back. There was a guy named Dougie who sometimes came to our neighbourhood and hung out with a couple of other guys. He also was picking on my younger brother, Junior, at school, even though Dougie was my size, but heavier. I had followed Dougie up the street one night and harassed him about bullying Junior.

One summer day, a few of us hung out in my front yard, kicking a soccer ball around. Dougie just happened to be there (he normally wasn't) and tried to get the ball off me. He kicked my leg on purpose, and it hurt. I finally kicked him back with my old cowboy boots. He then threw a punch at me. As we started to fight, Billy-Joe told us to stop it, but Ma said, 'Leave them alone, Billy-Joe.' Dougie and I started to really throw them. Robbie hollered, 'Kill him, Randy.'

As we traded punches, we gravitated towards a car in the driveway. Dougie was driven backwards. I landed a flurry of punches, but he hit me a couple of times towards the end that almost stopped me. I fought through it, though, and kept punching. I finally had him up against the car and landed shots at will. I asked him if he had enough. He said, 'Yes.' I had won!

I told him to not pick on Junior anymore. He went home.

Later that day, Dougie came back down Hinchey Avenue with his two buddies. They must have heard about the fight with me and couldn't believe that Dougie had lost. Dougie now had boots on. They hollered to me, wanting me to fight him again. I was watching Dennis in the back yard at the time. I yelled back that Dougie didn't really want to fight, but that *they* wanted him to. They huddled together for a minute and then went off in another direction. That was the end of it for good.

Not only was I tall and skinny, but I had bad teeth from years of neglect (and cigarettes & treats), and long scraggly hair. I was not exactly on every girl's wish list. In our hood, my close friends were considered handsome and cool. I was usually in last place — although I dated a girl occasionally. That would change when I joined the military, got my teeth fixed, and got in decent shape; kind of like *The Ugly Duckling* story.

My biggest goal at this time was to graduate. My friends had dropped out of BEC a long time ago. I now walked to school with Timmy Woodland and Tommy Head. We graduated together in '79. Timmy, Tommy and I also went to the prom together with our dates and spent the night at Lake Ainslie (without the girls). I think I made a bad pick for my prom date, as she spent most of the night making eyes at the handsome Timmy.

I wish I had asked the girl I actually had a crush on, but I was just too shy. I will never know if she would have said yes.

# Graduation

I have learned a lot in life since leaving home — like nothing ventured, nothing gained. I wish I knew that then.

In Grade 12, I won the BEC chess championship. The principal, Bryden MacDonald, called me into his office and presented me with the trophy — gold and red metal with a gold queen standing atop. He beamed at me, put his hand on my shoulder, grabbed the microphone and announced it to the whole school. That was an amazing moment in my life.

I really got into chess that year. I enjoyed studying chess books from the library about strategy. We played every Friday after school. Most of the chess club members were academic brainiacs. I enjoyed beating them. I remember one guy in particular, Andy, smashing the board and pieces against the wall when he realized that I was going to beat him down the board and turn my pawn into a Queen.

I fondly remember the long walk home from BEC on Fridays after school and chess. Sometimes it was raining or snowing. When I got home, Ma always gave me a warm plate of fish sticks, mashed potatoes and peas. I loved that meal and still do.

During that year, the BEC chess club competed in the Cape Breton Championship in Sydney. I did well in this tournament.

In one of my last games, the supervisor, who turned out to be the dad of my opponent, had to determine the winner of our game, as it was taking too long. After a lengthy deliberation, he concluded that his son would win. I am still unsure if it was the correct decision.

Anyway, they were both nice, so I accepted it. With that win, the son came in first or second, and I came in third.

A few days later, Ma found an article about the tournament in the *Cape Breton Post* and I cut it out. I was really happy with that achievement — third in all of Cape Breton.

Looking back, I think God gave me these little victories, which meant a lot to me, and gained significance after my prodigal life got straightened out.

I graduated from BEC in June '79. Ma threw a little party for me at the house and some of my friends and relatives dropped in to congratulate me. I received a few small presents. My brother Bradley came home from the Navy, which was great. Later that night, when I was pretty drunk, Bradley informed me that one of my friends was stealing beer from our basement, passing bottles out the window to another guy. I had a small argument with Bradley about it, but he was right.

After the party, when everyone had left, I sat on the back step and cried; maybe it was the stealing, or maybe it was just everything. I heard a soft female voice say to me, 'What's wrong, Randy.' I turned my head and saw Anna Drake up in the window. I had no answer. Outwardly, I had graduated and was joining the Canadian Forces; inwardly, I had no clue about life — maybe I was just starting to realize it.

After all, it was Ma's idea for me to join the military — to send money home to her like Bradley did. I wanted to be a veterinarian, but we couldn't afford university.

**Graduation**

Heck, we couldn't even afford a BEC ring or year book. Years later, my brother Junior found a yearbook at a garage sale and mailed it to me.

One morning, shortly before I left for the Forces, I got a call. Ma was in the Sydney jail. *How did she get there?* Donnie, who was now Ma's boyfriend, and I had to go pick her up. It was embarrassing. I think she was thrown in the slammer for mouthing off to a police officer.

Donnie was a good guy and I really liked him. He let me drive his old car shortly before I left home, straight down Hudson Street and into our driveway. Imagine, I was eighteen and this was the first time I had driven a car. We never owned one in all those years in New Waterford.

I had passed the Canadian Armed Forces tests and was able to pick the trade I wanted. I chose IS Tech (Integral Systems Technician) with the Air Force. Basically, this would entail working on electrical systems on aircraft — for example, autopilot, altimeters, airspeed indicators, and gyros.

I would soon be heading to CFB Cornwallis for basic training. I prepared by running and doing push-ups.

Was I ready to go out into the world? Well, I drank too much and smoked, had no clue about finances, driving a car, or life in general. And I was still a virgin. Catastrophe was right around the corner.

# 8

## *The Military Years*

Shortly after graduating, I took the train to CFB Cornwallis to begin basic training in the Canadian Forces. I was nervous, facing the unknown again, just like the eight-year-old in the car heading for Cape Breton.

Eleven weeks of basic training lay ahead of me. The first thing to go was my long hair! The new recruits are all called 'Alice' by the old recruits until they get their buzz cuts.

The new recruits were a mix of those who had some previous military training, like cadets and reservists, and people like me, who had none.

I loved the mess hall food — three great meals. After a few days, everyone received an advance on pay so we could buy the things we needed at the base store (Canex).

The main person in charge of our company was Master Corporal Payette, a tough army guy. He was of medium height with brown hair — stocky, tough, and fair. He was in excellent shape and could run well.

He called us 'reprobates' when hollering at us, which he did a lot. However, you learned after a while that he was doing things to test and improve you. I thought he was excellent.

We lived in a long barracks, with two beds to a section. I was paired with a tough and good chap named Trudeau. We did lots of marching exercises every day, learning all the basics: standing at attention, at ease, right wheel, left wheel, etc. We also learned to shoot rifles, machine guns and pistols. I loved that part. This included cleaning, taking them apart and re-assembly.

A major rule at the shooting range was to always keep your gun pointed down range, no matter what. One time while shooting, my rifle jammed. I put my arm up to signal to the master corporal monitoring us. He came over to check out my situation. Problem was, while examining my gun, I let it drift towards him. He grabbed the barrel, aimed it down range — and proceeded to give me the biggest tongue-lashing of my life – up one side of me and down the other. I never made that mistake again.

All the recruits were expected to pass certain benchmarks by the end of the course. For example: twenty-five push-ups, tread water for so many minutes and climb a rope to the top of the high gym ceiling. With my long and skinny arms, I couldn't do the push ups.

To help me out, Payette gave me extra push-ups every time I turned around. Normally, the boys got push-ups as punishments, but I got them for any excuse. For example, if we were waiting outside a building for a class, Payette would walk by: 'Thompson, give me twenty!' On one of the last days of our course, I completed the twenty-five push-ups as everyone cheered me on! Thank you, Master Corporal!

I was also weak in the water (strange for a young man who liked to play and swim in the Atlantic) and had to do extra time in the pool to accomplish the treading goal by the end.

Climbing the thick rope to the top was a real confidence booster as I was afraid of heights. They showed us a special technique to wrap our legs and feet around the rope so that we could propel ourselves up one body length at a time — using arms and legs. Towards the end of the course, we had to go all the way to the ceiling, touch the metal beam and come back down. I really couldn't believe I did it. It felt great.

We did a lot of running at Cornwallis – with rifle, gas mask and water canister. Towards the end of our time there, we heard about two hills we'd have to master after the ten-kilometre run. The final hill, and big one, was called Heartbreak Hill. I wasn't a fast runner, but running over time and distance didn't bother me.

Our company had an older guy, surnamed Scott, who couldn't make the big run. He was going to fail the course. Payette then did an amazing thing that I never forgot. He made some of us form a line behind Scott while running. One of us pushed him along, then peel off. Then the next guy would do the same, and so on, until Scott completed the entire distance! Well done, Master Corporal Payette!

## CAPE BRETON ORPHAN

By the end of our course, Payette had made me the right marker (the guy who keeps the pace on parade). On a blistering hot graduation day, we marched onto the scorching asphalt. Some guys fainted during the ceremony, but I endured. Ma, Bradley and Joy came down for the celebration, and we had coffee together afterwards.

After graduating basic training, I got posted to Ontario: CFB Kingston for basic electricity and then CFB Borden for aircraft courses. The training and food were top-notch. At night we went to the bars, especially on the weekends, where we often got hammered. I completed both courses by the first half of 1980.

Towards the end of my course at Borden, my friend John and I found out that we were posted to CFB Baden-Soellingen in West Germany. This was a choice four-year posting that everyone wanted, and the head instructor picked us. They had just started to allow privates to go overseas.

In my final month at Borden, I fell in love with a pretty brown-eyed classmate named Jenny. At a club dance one night, we had the last waltz together — which ended with a long kiss. We became instant boyfriend and girlfriend. We slept together that first night and a few days later, drove with another couple to the CN Tower in Toronto, where we had a fantastic time.

When our training came to an end, we said a tearful good-bye outside her barracks and promised to write and visit each other as soon as possible.

We were madly in love.

# 9

# *CFB Baden-Soellingen, West Germany*

Descending into CFB Lahr, Germany, I was amazed at the beauty of the countryside with its farming fields and greenery. After landing, I took the bus to Baden.

CFB Baden-Soellingen consisted of single level green buildings interspersed with trees and grass, blending in with the countryside for camouflage. There were multiple barracks for the men, and one for the women.

In the centre of the base stood a large Canex store. Cigarettes and alcohol were duty free. Other NATO members could also shop there, and it was quite humorous to watch the French load up on Canadian butter! Soon after I arrived, I bought a water colour painting from a German artist outside the Canex, which I still have — a painting of Neuschwanstein — the castle made more famous by Disney.

I started my German tour by working at 439 squadron on the CF-104 Starfighter — an old fighter jet that resembled a rocket with small wings. It was fast, powerful and loud!

It was hard, though, to concentrate on my new career with Jenny dominating my thoughts. I couldn't wait to get back to Ontario and the letter I had just received from her only stoked the flames.

After a couple of long months, I flew back to Canada to visit my love. I stayed at the CFB Trenton barracks, a place where visitors lodged. But much to my surprise, Jenny was nowhere to be found. I tracked down a friend of mine named Bart (who I met at basic training) and we had breakfast at the mess hall. I told him about my situation. He said he would look into it.

The next morning, I finally met Jenny in the underground tunnel connecting both sides of the base. She was on her way to work and greeted me with a wonderful smile. We embraced, kissed and she said we would meet after work. However, as afternoon turned into evening, she never showed up or called me. Something was definitely wrong. I tried to contact her many times over the next couple of days and finally went to her barracks. Nothing. Eventually I figured out she was avoiding me. I was devastated.

I still had a whole week left at Trenton, before my flight back, and didn't really know what to do, so I spent my time playing pool at a club on base. Bart visited me a couple of times, and finally suggested that Jenny may have a new boyfriend.

A day or two later, while I played pool, Jenny and a female friend suddenly showed up. They wore his-and-hers t-shirts, which seemed to suggest they had boyfriends. Jenny didn't even talk to me, but turned away.

## CFB Baden-Soellingen

I was crushed and lost — the orphan again.

I put the pool cue down and walked out of the club, and headed back to my room. It was a long walk. A guy asked me for money on the way, I gave him twenty bucks. Back at the room, I took some pills and tried to kill myself. Shortly thereafter, I walked down to the front desk and told the receptionist that they should call an ambulance. I was already feeling high and strange. I climbed the stairs to my room. A moment later, two plainclothes police officers burst in and searched my room, asking me questions — trying to find out what I had taken. Then the ambulance arrived and rushed me to the hospital, where they pumped my stomach. It was a painful, horrible experience.

I survived, but it was a close call. A very kind nurse sat with me throughout the night (as I threw up repeatedly and recovered). She explained to me that there are more fish in the sea. I never forgot that. Bart found out and rebuked Jenny for what she had done. He told me that afterwards. A few days later, a hospital psychiatrist talked to me to ensure I was okay, then sent me back to Germany.

*Life lesson*: Don't isolate yourself. Reach out for help. Pray.

You know the song, *Lean on Me*? Lean on someone.

Once back in Germany, I told my friend, John, that I had tried to end it all. He replied, 'Let's go have a beer.' So, we did. I'm sure we got drunk. We always did. Many guys in the Forces were alcoholics, and I would become one too. That seemed to be the solution for everything — get hammered.

## CAPE BRETON ORPHAN

No matter what we did in Germany at this time, whether on the base or in the German towns, we were constantly drinking. We drank each day after work at the club, and more on the weekends — especially when there was always a beer tent or wine fest to visit.

The Jenny event quickly faded from my life. I would now embark on a four-year tour of drinking and chasing women. I had filled out, had my teeth fixed and of course, had a nice short haircut. Some women were actually interested in me. Just maybe, I wasn't the Ugly Duckling anymore. And the saying was true: there were more fish in the sea. Lots of fish.

The 104 had a single engine which made a great afterburner light in the night sky, although we worked mainly in the day. The plane was nicknamed the widow-maker because it crashed a lot — having only one engine and small wings.

There were ejections and crashes during my time in Baden, including a German 104 that crashed close to the base the first year I arrived. A pilot died in that one. Two German jets attacked the base for an exercise, and it was one of the loudest things I have ever heard — one of them roared right over my barracks room. I hit the deck! As they kept attacking, one of them clipped the other one causing the crash.

I was able to walk to the squadron from my living quarters each morning. Sometimes I got picked up by passing motorists — whether officers or lower ranks — most of them in high end German cars, like BMW's.

The squadrons (441, 421 and 439) were each laid out in a circular fashion with hardened aircraft shelters (HAS's) dotting the asphalt.

The pilots had their own building and would come into our shack to sign out an aircraft. The sergeant manned the counter and dealt directly with the pilots. Two techs (normally wearing a ball cap, white t-shirt and tool belt) would already be at the concrete HAS with the electrical hooked up and ready to go. We always had a front-end man (or woman) and a rear man. Our job was to get the pilot headed towards the runway — safely and quickly. The pilots were normally on their way to the range.

Most of the time, I was the front-end man and would help to strap in the pilot and close all the electronic panels. By hand signals, standing at the front of the plane — where the pilot and the rear guy could see me, I would go through the start-up. The forced air would be turned on and the plane fired up.

Things got loud!

When going under the wings to check things, you always had to hold onto the leading edge with one hand because they were so sharp they could cut you bad. We also wore a baseball cap for extra protection, and, of course, ear defenders!

Once through the steps, we would marshal the pilot on his way. We also received the jets when they returned and shut them down and helped the pilots out. We would then do an after-flight check, and refuel the jets. Sometimes we got a rush job when a pilot was late for the range and we dashed out to the tarmac and got them out in record speed.

I loved working at the squadron and quickly gained the favour of Sergeant Meindl, who was an excellent boss. I also learned to drive (finally!) and tow aircraft. I had great teachers. Many of the guys treated me like a son or brother and the squadron was like a family.

After six months, we, the new privates, had to rotate through other departments — such as Labs where we fixed electronic cards inside black boxes and such things. I didn't like Labs as it was all inside work: clean and quiet. The men there seemed more concerned with the appearance of their uniforms than anything else. We spent a lot of time sitting around, tweaking resistors and playing cards at lunch. I would much rather be outside.

I then rotated to Snags, where we repaired the fighters. We worked on the autopilot, altimeters, airspeed indicators, gyros, and other systems. Much to my surprise, I really enjoyed it. Snags work was brain work — figuring out where the defect was in the system and fixing it. It was detective work: whether repairing or replacing a black box or tracking down and fixing a broken wire.

We also tried to fix black boxes at Snags by hooking them up to the gigantic UG 1000 – a massive yellow computerized machine with blinking green lights that would 'fly' the black box and figure out where the problem was. We sometimes switched out a card from inside the black box and tried it again or sent the box to Labs.

As part of NATO, we had to get X amount of aircraft

ready each night. Sometimes that meant staying after midnight to get a plane serviceable. There was a day shift and a night shift, which rotated. I had great bosses (master corporals) in Ralph, Ted and Mark. I started working for Ralph and Ted and then later worked for Mark.

I did very well at Snags. My bosses again liked me and eventually I ran a small crew of a few men. Mark, who was my master corporal, was away at hockey (because he was a top player on the base team) a lot in the winter, and depended on me.

Once a year our department (in this case Electrical and IS Techs) wrote up a report on each person called a PER: performance evaluation report. These reports were used for promotions and postings. Sergeant Simpson called me into his office one day and read mine to me. I couldn't believe my ears. I thought he was talking about someone else. My master corporals had praised me through the roof. If I hadn't been turning into such a drunk, I could have done very well in the military and stayed in for a long time. However, the skills I acquired would come in handy down the road.

Over time, I gathered a large number of friends at the base and we partied a lot, especially on the weekends. We called ourselves the Knights of the Round Table, as we seemed to gather at this one table at the Ambassador Lounge. Looking back, I wonder if some of the guys were true friends or just drinking buddies.

We drank so much that we were smashed before we drove off the base to the beer tents.

After a while I discovered Asbach, a strong German brandy, and would get obliterated on that late at night. Some of my friends got into hash. I smoked it occasionally with my friends, but was never a big drug user.

By early 1983, I was living in a beautiful town named Iffezheim, where I rented a nice one-bedroom apartment from a wonderful German family, who I became friends with. I had also gotten myself a snazzy blue Peugeot 504 car, purchased from John. Iffezheim was also home to the Festhall, a building where we used to party during Fasching.

One night, after another heavy drinking session, I stumbled out of the hall. I only lived a few blocks away, but just had to drive home. Close to my house, I swerved around a corner and smashed into a parked car. I think I might have fallen asleep behind the wheel. So, being really smart, I now drove all the way to my friend Doug Saunders's house in Hugelsheim, a town close to the base. The Colonel was his nickname.

I parked the car, knocked on the door and The Colonel let me crash on his couch. Some time later, the door buzzer went off and Doug answered. It was the Polizei. He explained that no one else was there and they could come in and check. They did and there I was. They had followed the oil leaking from my car, all the way to his house. About a week later, after getting busted and losing my license, a young German man showed me a photo of the accident in the local paper. I was deeply ashamed.

What a great ambassador for Canada I had become.

# 10

## *German Flames*

One thing that saved me in Germany was fastball, which some people call softball. I played for the 439 squadron team the first year (and we won our league!) and the second year tried out for The Baden Raiders, the base all-star team.

During one of the tryouts for the Raiders, the coach stood with the catcher and made a line-up of the players, facing him. When I got to the front of the line, the coach tried to hit the ball past me. I gobbled it up and threw it to the catcher. After a couple of times through the line with the other players, it was my turn again.

After scooping the ball and throwing it in, the coach told me to stay put. He then hit another one and then another one. He hit them harder each time and in more difficult to reach spots – but he couldn't hit the ball past me. I snagged each one.

Later that day, the coach told me that I had made the team.

I owe that performance to a practice I used to do at Central school in New Waterford. I used to throw a rubber baseball (remember the red, white and blue ones?) off the big wall at the back of the school, close to where we played baseball. I did this fun practice all by myself, when there were no games going on. I would throw the ball faster and faster and try to get it past myself, but I got to most of them. I just loved doing that drill, and it paid big dividends!

I loved playing for the Raiders, who wore blue uniforms with white trim and lettering. I got to wear my favourite number — 7. I was not a great hitter, especially against top-notch pitching, but I was a pretty good fielder — playing second base the first year and shortstop after that.

The Raiders travelled around Germany and played US teams close to our area: Frankfurt, Giessen, Essen, Karlsruhe, and others. The Americans were excellent ballplayers and the tournaments were fun. We usually finished around third place or so. Once we got close to the semi-finals, we faced excellent pitching and heavy hitters that were a step up from us.

However, one year, in Vicenza, Italy, at a big US Fourth of July tournament, we actually won. Del, our third-baseman, got the big hit and I scored the winning run from second. We each received a case containing a large golden medal lying on blue velvet. It was the nicest prize I ever won.

Once again, the baseball was great, but the drinking that surrounded it was overboard. The coach, Kip, who was a recovering alcoholic, pleaded with us not to drink at night before the championship game. This was the first time we listened to him. We got drunk on the long bus ride home from Italy to Baden, though. We thought we were big heroes.

My partying life was spiralling out of control. Each year became worse and worse. I drank so much beer, whiskey, and Ausbach, that I actually started to black out. Sometimes, I would wake up in my car, having passed out in the early morning hours and had no recollection of what happened the night before. It affected all areas of my life: not washing my clothes regularly, not eating properly (my fridge usually contained hot dogs and beer). I only ate well when eating out. I was also smoking like a chimney. It all started to catch up to me.

One year, the Canadian Forces National Championship for fastball was hosted by CFB Gagetown in New Brunswick. So, afterwards, I could visit the Cape if I wanted to, but I chose not to, and just returned to Germany. I didn't tell Ma that I would be close to home. Ma and Dennis were by now living with another man and out of the Low Rentals. This guy turned out to be violent also and threatened Ma with a broken plate. I didn't know the full details, but it was depressing to hear about. Nothing seemed to change there, and maybe I was just so tired of it, I finally tuned out. Eventually, Ma and Dennis got their own place on 2nd Street.

My first couple of years in the military, I travelled home for Christmas.

The first year, I bought Ma *The Four Seasons* by Norman Rockwell, which was four separate paintings. She loved that artist. The next Christmas, my duffel bag was taken by mistake by another Forces guy, so I didn't have my personal belongings or presents. During my visits, I spent more time with Jake — drinking — than with Ma and the family.

## *Sardinia, Italy*

The Air Force was involved in a NATO exercise in 1982, close to the city of Cagliari in Sardinia, Italy. I was chosen to go with Snags. At the military airport (Decimomannu) we carried out special Air Weapons Training.

The working conditions were very hot. At night, we drank a lot of Sambuca, beer and other liquor. Late one night, at the barracks, I ended up in a room with some guys I didn't know. We were gabbing and drinking. Sean, a husky older ex-Army type, and I sat alone at a small round table. While talking, he began to slowly move bottles out of the way. I wasn't really paying attention. Out of the blue, he punched me in the face and I flew backwards.

I stood up, but he cowered by his bed. I shouted, 'What the hell are you doing?' but didn't try to punch him. His room-mate intervened and I left to go to my room, thinking the bizarre encounter was over. I made the big mistake of stopping at the community bathroom to wash up. When I came out, guess who was standing in the hallway?

'I heard what you said,' he said, and came at me again.

I didn't want to fight, but had no choice. I hit him with a couple of good shots, but he just kept coming. Eventually he got me into a headlock and started punching me in the face. I couldn't free myself. My blood dripped onto the floor. I hollered at him to stop. He finally did, as guys rushed out of their rooms, into the hallway. They separated us and I walked back to my room.

My roommate, Jeff, was out at the time, but when he returned, he looked at me and said, 'What the hell happened to you?' My face was pretty smashed up.

I decided to go for a long walk. I left the base and after a while came across a little church. The door was unlocked, so I entered and sat down in a rear pew. It was empty and dark. I just sat there. Sometimes there are no words. After a while, I left.

Looking back, I believe that short visit to the church was significant, as many things were about to unfold over the next few years.

On the way back to the base, far behind, a bunch of wild dogs ran after me. I hurried up to make it back safely, but I had to be careful. The base had tight security and they had shot someone a few years before.

That night I had a vivid dream. I saw a glowing white light with greenish tinge in the middle of a large room. I stood upon a stair structure and three or four women stood on either side of me in white clothing. When I woke up, I wondered about the dream. Did it mean something? It was as if they were my wives.

In the morning, I had to go through the humiliation of my colleagues seeing me with a black eye and fat lip. It was hard to go to breakfast at the mess hall and have everyone stare and whisper. However, a few months later I felt better when I saw Sean back at Baden, and he was sporting a black eye courtesy of a Raiders' teammate.

## *Katie*

I met Katie in the summer of 1983 at the Ambassador Lounge on the base. She was in her late teens, and, along with her parents, visiting her sister Marilyn — a military friend of mine. Katie was pretty with mid-length brunette hair and brown eyes.

I was playing a lot of baseball that summer and had just returned from a tournament. I found out that Katie had briefly dated another one of Marilyn's friends, but that had quickly ended. When I found out she was free, I asked her out.

Katie met me at the ball park after a practice. I now had my driver's license back, and drove us to a small Gasthaus in Iffezheim, where we had a meal and a few drinks. I had a *Wiener Schnitzel mit Bratkartoffeln*, and I think Katie ate a Cordon Bleu. We had a great time chatting and laughing. Later, we went to my apartment, which was close by. She spent the night.

Katie soon returned to Victoria, BC with her parents. As an aside, but important note, Katie's parents and Marilyn were heavy drinkers,

During the intervening nine months, Katie and I stayed

in touch by letters and phone calls. Those were the days when you had to have a ton of change and sit in a little phone booth and keep plugging coins in during the call, the operator prompting you.

Katie surprised me in 1984 by sending me a gigantic Valentine's Day card with a racing car theme. I opened it at the post office, and chuckled as the love needle went to full. I brought it to the club and one of my *friends* saw it lying on the table and said (into the air, but directed at me), 'Why do all the jerks get the girls.'

I smiled.

## *Bad Drug Trip*

Late in the summer of '83, some of the guys tried acid at a concert. We attended rock concerts often during my tour of Germany. I tried acid once during a beer tent festival. It was weird, but didn't give me a bad reaction. However, one night at a party by a swimming quarry, a *friend* slipped a hit of acid (and maybe more) into my beer, without my knowledge. It was the same guy who had dated Katie before me. I had a very bad trip that night and seriously thought I was going to die.

The Colonel helped me that night, or should I say morning, as we were up until sunrise. I was outside, leaning against the house wall as I talked with my friend. How bad was the trip? I pooped my pants and honestly felt like I was going to die. Thanks to God, once again, I survived. To this day, I guard my drinks, and would advise everyone to. It is absolute evil to do that to someone. The Colonel admonished my 'friend' for that.

## CAPE BRETON ORPHAN

The Colonel told me recently that his drink had also been tampered with.

*Another life lesson*: Don't go along with the crowd. If you don't want to do drugs, or anything else, don't do them! Stand your ground and find new friends.

In March, 1984, I was working the night shift at the Snags hanger. It was closing time, around midnight, and we were doing some final checks. The hangar was full with jets, as we packed them in at the end of the night. I walked through the hangar, close to the main office where we signed our paperwork. I was just about to walk on one side of a fighter, when I changed my mind and chose the other side to go into the office, and off the hangar floor.

At that moment, something blew off and a tech shouted, 'Fire! Fire! Fire!' I looked under the jet, right beside me, and could see flames spreading on the ground on just the other side — *right where I would have been*. The safety systems guys had accidentally blown off a wing tip fuel tank. Someone grabbed a fire extinguisher off the wall, but the fire was too big.

I ran into the office.

People were scrambling and running everywhere it seemed. The fire got real bad, real fast. I remember going around the building and re-entering the Electrical Shop. I phoned my friend, Ross, who was working in Supply that night — right across the street. He got out. I also phoned the fire department.

Those in charge soon gathered us outside the Snags hangar on one side, but there were glass windows towards the top of the building that could shatter — so they quickly moved us far away to the runway. The leaders organized a volunteer crew, together with the fire department, and those guys — courageously — went back into that hangar with a very long hose and tried to put the fire out. An ejection seat blew through the roof and some rounds were fired from a jet (because things were over-heating).

Unbelievably, they did it! They put that fire out. The next day, when they examined the damage, some aircraft were almost burned through their skin, they had been so close to blowing up. They were fully fuelled and full of liquid oxygen. It was a miracle that one didn't explode. One plane going off would have blown up all the jets in the building, with everything and everyone.

I was pretty shaken up like everyone else. It was the Fasching season on the base. I went to a club and then went home and looked for something more to drink. The base emergency siren had gone off and most came in to help. They also wanted everyone to come in the next day and clean up, but I just stayed home. I think I was in shock.

Once in a while I think about that fire and I think about how I changed my mind in a millisecond and walked to the office instead of the other direction. *Thank you, Lord.*

### *Promotion to Corporal*

In order to get promoted to corporal, I needed to pass my Trade Qualification Exam. This last step was a big national test for all IS Techs — happening at the same time.

There were giant trade books to study and my bosses gave me the time I needed. I studied well over the months and thought I had passed my test.

When my official mark came in, I had failed. *Great.* That meant I would have to do all that studying again and re-take the test. I was summoned to the Chief Warrant Officer's office. This is the highest rank of non-commissioned officers, and this position and badge strikes fear into most service members, including officers!

CWO Ford went up one side of me and down the other, rebuking me for failing the test, and questioning everything about my life and service.

However, a month or so later, as I was in the middle of my studies again, a surprising letter came in for me, copied to all my bosses. I had passed the original test! Somehow, we had all taken the wrong test, so they had boosted everyone's mark — except for three of us, who had been missed.

A wonderful man at Air Force Headquarters at CFB Winnipeg, had found the mistake and corrected it! Yes! No more studying for me! Days later, they called me and another member onto the hangar floor and presented us with our corporal stripes.

I was now Corporal Thompson.

## *Return to Canada*

One day I came into Snags and my boss, Mark, handed me my posting letter. I opened it by my locker. This would determine my next four year posting.

I could have asked for an extension to Germany, as many guys did, but I wanted to return to Canada. I was really hoping to get either CFB Greenwood, Nova Scotia or CFB Summerside, PEI.

My heart sank! I was posted to CFB Shearwater, Nova Scotia. This was the last place on earth I wanted. Shearwater was a Navy posting with Sea King (known as Sea Pig) helicopters, and sometimes the Air Force guys had to go out to sea for long stretches. With Katie in mind, I hated the thought of going there.

However, after seeing my sad reaction, Mark handed me another letter — my *real* posting — not the fake one they had doctored. *Not nice, guys*!

In hindsight, it was a terrible prank. There are some things you shouldn't mess with. A career posting is one of them.

Next stop would be CFB Greenwood, Nova Scotia. But first, a short vacation to Victoria, BC, to visit Katie.

# 11

## *CFB Greenwood*

In May of 1984, I returned to Canada. I ordered a cheese and pepperoni pizza my first night back. I had really missed Canadian pizza! The next day I flew out to visit Katie.

Katie lived at her parents' house in a suburb called Langford. Each day we drove her dad to work, at the Navy dockyard, and then had the car for ourselves. Victoria and Vancouver Island reminded me of Cape Breton, being so green and beautiful, with similar trees, hills, and of course, the ocean. One of the places that we visited was popular Goldstream Park, famous for its salmon run. It was there, on a small wooden bridge, that I asked Katie to marry me. She said, 'Yes!'

Time flew by, and soon I had to head out to Nova Scotia.

After arriving at CFB Greenwood, I rented a small apartment off base in a sleepy town called Middleton. I neither liked the country pace nor my work, which consisted of working on Lab equipment — high tech machines that flew the INU (inertial navigation units) of the Aurora aircraft. Looking back, the real problem was most likely my bad attitude and the distance away from Katie. She visited me once in Greenwood, and together we went to Halifax to see my dad, who now lived there.

My first year in Germany, when I went home for Christmas, I found out that Dad had recently moved to Halifax.

On my return trip, I was going to stay for a night with him. After arriving, I waited for him in the Halifax bus station, but he was late. An hour or so later, a small scruffy man, asleep on a large garbage container close to me, stirred and got up. It was my dad. I couldn't believe it. We then walked to his place as he didn't own a car.

We had supper at his dingy one-bedroom apartment, in an older building, and then he took me to a bar for a couple of drinks. On the way back, he asked me if I wanted to fight him. Of course, I said, 'No,' but it was bizarre. He was still as unstable as ever.

Dad worked as a window-washer on high-rise buildings. It wasn't surprising that he could do this risky work as he used to jump out of aircraft. However, his love of heights was not passed on to me.

While stationed in Greenwood, I had a few short visits, and then never saw him again.

One night, in 1984, I drank at the club on the base and drove home.

Just outside the base gates the police pulled me over and nailed me for drinking and driving.

I had to go to court and lost my licence, but I handed in my German one and kept the Canadian one. I continued to drive my car and no one was the wiser (for now).

My sergeant placed me on a Life Skills course (basically an AA program) because of the drinking and driving.

At first, I wasn't happy about it, but this turned out to be a blessing in disguise. I also put in my release around this time, which meant I had six months left in the Forces.

The first day in the Life Skills class, which was in Halifax, everyone sat on chairs in a circle. As each person introduced themselves, they said their name, followed by, '*I'm an alcoholic.*'

When it came to me, I only said my name, like some of the other new people did. However, within a few days, I said, 'Hi. My name is Randy, and *I'm an alcoholic.*'

One of the goals of the course was to go the whole thirty days and have not even one beer. If so, they awarded you with a blue poker chip signifying the accomplishment.

The teachers of the course — a few guys, including an older man named Tom — were phenomenal and caring.

I remember one time them giving us this thought: *Could we go to a bar and only have one beer*? I remember thinking, why would you go a bar and only have one beer? It was a foreign concept to me. But the lights started to go on.

Tom also said one day, 'You don't have to wait until the elevator is on the bottom floor before you get off.' Another nugget of wisdom that I have hung on to and shared in my life.

One day, the teachers asked us to talk a little about our families. I listened as each person gave their story, but became apprehensive as my turn approached. When it came to me, I couldn't say a word. Tears welled up.

The teacher graciously recognized my predicament and asked the next person to speak.

I knew right then and there that I had a giant problem in my life. At the end of the course, I received the blue poker chip for going thirty days without drinking. I will always remember that accomplishment, and wish I had it today. This was a big turning point in my life, and even though I drank again afterwards, I always had that achievement to fall back on.

As I got closer to my Canadian Forces release date, one of the sergeants at work said that I would pull it (meaning reverse my decision). He made a comment like, once you're in the Forces you can't leave; they have too big a hold on your life. But I was serious and knew that I was leaving for good.

In April 1985, I left the military, taking off my shirt and tie as I drove out the front gate of the base for the final time. I quickly loaded up my car, took what little money I had and headed for Calgary, where Ross and Marilyn, now married, lived. They were both Supply Techs posted to the Army base. The plan was for Katie to meet me at her sister's house.

The reason why I didn't have much money when I left the Forces was that the bank manager at Greenwood, who also owned my apartment building, had scooped all my pension money to pay off my car — the horrendous car I had bought from a used car salesman. It was a Plymouth Horizon TC-3 with a bad engine that broke down shortly after I bought it. And if that wasn't bad enough, one night it broke down with Katie in the car as we drove back from Halifax to Greenwood. I think it was close to another $2,000 to get a rebuilt engine put in. So, the few thousand dollars I would have got upon retirement — was gone!

A great start to my new civilian life.

I now got the crazy idea to race through Canada. I would just nap in my car. This would save me lots of money. I got through Nova Scotia, New Brunswick and Quebec with ease. Overtired and speeding through Ontario, I was pulled over by the Ontario Provincial Police. *How stupid was I?* My license was still officially suspended. Everything I owned was in that car. It was packed with just enough room for me to drive.

I still had my Canadian license and handed that to the officer. He strolled back to his car and then returned five minutes later. I was sweating, thinking how in the world would I get out of this? My car would be left in Ontario with all I owned. I didn't have enough money to handle anything like that. It would be a nightmare. The officer told me that my license was suspended. I explained, with a straight face, that it was my German license that was suspended (on the military base), but that my normal license was good. Something like that.

He went back to his car again to check out my fable, and after a *very* long time, walked back to my car.

## CAPE BRETON ORPHAN

He said that he was trying to get confirmation that my license was suspended, but it was *Easter Sunday* and he couldn't get ahold of anyone. Unbelievably, he let me go, and I drove away. He followed me for a long time; maybe fifteen minutes or so, and then he finally peeled off.

What a miracle. Looking back, there's no doubt in my mind that God was blessing me, despite my stupidity and hardships, and wanted me to go out west.

# 12

## Go West, Young Man

A few days later, I arrived at Ross and Marilyn's house at CFB Calgary. They were very hospitable and put me up. Soon the drinks were flowing and the barbecue was fired up. Katie showed up a couple of days later and life was great.

Ross was like a brother. There was a big field behind their house and we'd go out and throw the football around and chat. The four of us went out dancing a couple of times also. Looking back, the big problem, ever-present, was the excessive drinking each day.

Katie and I stayed in Calgary for a month or two, but the plan was to have our wedding in Edmonton, because Brad and Alison and their spouses now lived there.

We ended up moving to Edmonton also, where I got a temporary job installing car stereos.

Every Friday night, we played cards for small money, and even though I thought myself a good card player, the other couples took about twenty dollars from us each time, which we couldn't afford. Katie had just received a settlement from a car accident that happened when she was a teen, and she dipped into that to help pay the rent and buy things.

Katie and I took a four-week marriage course at a historical Anglican church, and walked down the aisle in early August. Katie was pregnant and our first child was due in March, '86. After a couple of months, I got laid off from the stereo store. Ed, Katie's dad, was a major influence in her life (she being his only biological child out of four children), and he soon worked on her to return to Victoria. So we did.

In Victoria, I took on landscaping jobs, but couldn't find anything meaningful. In March, Katie went into labour and we rushed to the hospital.

She had a very hard time with the birth of Jason, and because the nurse had explained the lights and indicators on the machine hooked up to her, I knew that Katie and the baby were in trouble.

In the hallway, I confronted the doctor who seemed to be moving way too slow. I hit the wall beside him while expressing my concerns. Shortly thereafter, they did an emergency C-section. Mom and baby came through just fine, although Jason ended up with a little pointy head, covered up with a cap. It was quite an amazing feeling to hold my first child.

Later that year, John (my friend from Germany) and his wife, Joyce, dropped down to Victoria, and later we visited them up at their new posting in CFB Comox.

Through some old military connections, I was offered a civilian job working on planes in Churchill, Manitoba. We thought it was a good opportunity. I would go out first, and then later, the family.

However, when I got to Calgary, I decided that I didn't want to continue on to Churchill, which is very far north and isolated. Maybe it was just intuition, but I felt very comfortable in Calgary.

I rented an apartment, and Katie and Jason soon joined me, Ed driving them out.

Initially, I found work as a security guard and Katie was hired as a nanny, but my work was not really a career.

At one point we had to go on Social Assistance, which turned out to be a blessing in disguise, as they put me on a short job-finding course. I approached some aircraft maintenance companies at the airport and much to my surprise landed a good job at Field Aviation. They were a growing maintenance company with military contracts. It was right up my alley. Ed helped me to buy some tools to get started, as the techs there all had their own, unlike the Air Force.

At Field Aviation, we worked on military planes like the Twin Otter and Buffalo. We also serviced civilian aircraft like the Dash 8 and Fokker, working out of a giant hangar with around two hundred employees.

Katie and I were able to afford more things now. I remember her being so happy to get a new blue love seat and sofa. I had bought a second hand one, shortly before, but it was so bad, she ordered me to return it!

## CAPE BRETON ORPHAN

We then moved a couple of times and finally rented a nice townhouse in the northeast, close to the airport. We really liked Calgary. By this time, I was a Flames and Stampeders fan.

In early '87, Ma came out for a visit. We paid for it out of Katie's settlement money. Ma was only at our place for a day or two and spent most of her time in the kitchen, drinking tea and smoking.

Each night, at bed time, we rocked Jason to sleep in the living room. He had a habit of making a cute moaning sound that helped him fall asleep.

One night, Ma complained from the kitchen, 'Why is he making that sound?'

It was hard to believe. She had barely seen her new grandson and was already complaining about him. I replied, 'Ma, it's his house, and this is the sound he makes.'

Within a day or two, Ma decided it was time to go to Edmonton and visit Brad and Alison. Ma would spend most of her time up there and return to Calgary just before leaving for home. We felt used.

I think if we had stayed in our townhouse for about three to five years, we would have been okay, but Katie's girlfriend from Victoria, who also lived in Calgary, had just purchased a new house. At the time, the government offered a five percent down payment to get people into new homes. Katie really wanted to buy, and at this time there was tremendous growth in the northeast by the airport.

Ed had promised Katie another five percent on top

of the government's. So, we began house-hunting and eventually found one in Martindale, a new neighbourhood in the northeast. It was a nice two-level house on a cul-de-sac. But just to show how tight it all was, we couldn't even afford to have a bay window when it was being built, which was an extra five hundred dollars.

We bought the new house for around $80,000. However, with only me working and a second child on the way, financial pressure was building. On top of that, we both drank and smoked — going through a pack of cigarettes each a day. We were young and foolish.

In July '87, a crew from Field Aviation was sent to Salisbury, Maryland to work for De Havilland on the Dash 8 aircraft doing an electrical modification. It was great work. We knew it well and these out-of-town trips provided extra income for my employer and the techs.

Our new baby boy wasn't due till September, so I was picked to go with the crew.

We stayed at a nice hotel as usual, and, as usual, I drank too much each night and was hung over most days.

After a couple of weeks, I was stunned when my colleagues walked into the hotel bar with balloons. Casey had arrived early! It was early August and Field Aviation rushed me home.

When I arrived at the Calgary hospital, it was quite a sight to see Casey — looking pretty giant and healthy — in the premature ward with all the other miniature babies. Although his lungs were underdeveloped, mom and baby were doing just fine.

## CAPE BRETON ORPHAN

As far as work, I really liked my co-workers: Bryan, Spencer, Roberto, Graham, and 'the Chief' — Bob, our Scottish boss. My work skills were improving, and much to my surprise, I got a huge compliment from the Canadian Forces pilots for a lighting modification I had done on the instrument panel for a Twin Otter.

I also got a big pat on the back from the main supervisor at Field Aviation for the work done in Maryland (which included breaking up a potential fist-fight between two colleagues — Canadians in action!). I worked mainly with Bryan, who was an excellent tech and good friend. I used to go to his house to watch Flames' games and he would pick me up for rec ice hockey on Friday nights in the winter.

In '88 we had another out of town trip to do the same electrical mod on the Dash 8's in Halifax, Nova Scotia. We had a couple of days off at one point, and I was able to jump on a plane for a short visit with Ma. That was the last time we were together until Dennis's wedding in '99.

Although I had a well-paid union job, the financial pressures grew through the years.

Sometimes, shortly before pay day, we would have to return a couple of packs of smokes to the store to buy some food.

There were also lots of parties in our cul-de-sac as it was made up of young couples our age, and it was always someone's birthday. One guy, Hal, was about ten years older than most of us, and he drank a lot of whiskey. Sometimes, I had the odd drink with him.

Hal got so drunk one night, he fell into brick barrier surrounding the bonfire. *Great.* Now I was friends with a bunch of civilian alcoholics, and was still one myself.

One evening at home, in '89, I walked down the stairs. At the bottom, I suddenly felt light-headed and had sharp chest pains. I entered the living room, which was kind of spinning.

'I feel weird,' I said. I lay down on the floor and Katie phoned the ambulance. I was rushed in and hooked up to the heart monitors. Everything checked out well and they released me a few hours later. Katie had stayed at home with the kids, and a couple of friends came over to sit with her.

Although I was technically fine, it shook me up. I was *afraid* — afraid of dying. Over the next few months, which would turn into years, every once in a while, I would get a sharp pain in my chest — right in the heart area. And it always scared me. The doctors could never find out what was causing it. They checked one time for an ulcer, but it was negative. One female doctor suggested that it might be mental, but I knew it was a real physical thing.

I learned over time that my health issue was related to my diet, and no doubt to the smoking and drinking. Every day for lunch at Field Aviation, I ate a big plate of fries covered in gravy, washed down with a coke. My problems were partly caused by acid reflux. A doctor told me to quit smoking immediately, which was the right thing, for sure. Over the years this health problem improved, but would still reappear from time to time.

This was God's wake-up call on my life. I was only twenty-eight years old and not ready to die. Another interesting thing surrounding this event, is that one year, when I was a kid, we got an Ouija board for Christmas in Low Point. We asked it all kinds of questions, including when we would die. For me, it came out as twenty-eight.

And even though the prediction was not responsible for my health issue that night, it was something I had occasionally thought about as I got closer to my birthday. However, I can honestly say that I did not think about it that night. Regardless, I would never have an Ouija board, or anything like it, in my house.

Another interesting fact, is that Ma smashed that board over my head that year in Low Point. I can't remember why, but yeah, I broke the Ouija board.

# 13

## *What is Truth?*

Shortly after my health problems started, we were visited by Mormons. The two young men, with sharp suits and short hair, who came to our door, told us they were elders. They were clean and sparkly and had a 'message for families.'

Over the next six months we went to their church. They frequently visited the house and were so kind and got us plugged in to their church. One of the ways that Mormons work is to help you in any way they can. They will get you work if possible (with one of their members), they will help renovate your house, they will visit you, etc. One time they got Flames hockey tickets, and took Jason and me to a game.

During this time, and unbeknownst to me, Katie was secretly talking to her Aunt Mable, a Pentecostal, about the Mormons — aka The Church of Jesus Christ of Latter-Day Saints. Mable had given her a book, written by an ex-Mormon, and it was filled with vital information about their cultish practises. Katie started to ask me tough questions.

I, in turn, asked my sponsor (the guy working on me from their church) tough questions. One such question was, are black people allowed to be priests in the Mormon church?

Alan said, 'I saw a man baptized last week, and he was as black as the ace of spades.' But, as I found out soon, this answer was a side-tracking lie.

The Mormons did *not* allow black people to hold their 'priesthood' until the 1970s — when they faced big public pressure over the issue. Amazingly, their 'modern day prophet' then got a revelation (supposedly from God) — and blacks were suddenly allowed to hold the priesthood. The Mormons had been around since the 1800s, and were pretty racist for a long time. I researched it for myself.

The more I researched this 'church' the crazier I found it: their strange teachings, the bizarre rituals at their 'temples', and their violent, secretive past.

Over time, I concluded that they were indeed a cult. *Great.* I had just gotten baptized there. The Mormon experience was significant, though, as it drove me to the Bible to find out the truth for myself. All I knew was that the King James Bible was true. So, I started to read it for myself. *Every day.*

In late '89, Katie's mother, Sheila, had a stroke. I took the call and had to break it to Katie when she came home. Katie flew out to Victoria immediately, and a day or two later, I drove the boys out. Sheila was in bad shape at the hospital, and the family took turns sleeping in her room to always have someone there.

During this time in Victoria, I had one final struggle with Mormonism. I got the Mormon book again and read it and wondered if it was true. However, one day at Katie's parents' house, I was reading the New Testament, when a verse from the gospel of Matthew popped out at me. Jesus was talking about false prophets at the end of time, and it seemed to point at Joseph Smith the founder and 'prophet' of the Mormons. It was like God was speaking to me by his Spirit.

Katie's dad used to make a good bonfire in an old metal drum beside his house. One night there was a big fire and I threw in all the Mormon books I had. And that was the end of that, for good!

Reading the Bible became the greatest thing in my life. I felt such a peace when I read. It also brought me joy, strength and wisdom, things that I was severely lacking. I really had no true wisdom in my life before this. My parents and teachers didn't impart any deep wisdom to me. Yes, we got little nuggets of knowledge from time to time, but nothing like this. The teachings of Jesus were incredible. The Book of Proverbs, wonderful.

The Bible itself showed that these groups (like Jehovah's Witnesses and Mormons) were cults, and contradicted their false teachings. For example, the New Testament (and Old Testament) clearly showed that God made and loves people of all nations. There is no way that God would prevent black people from becoming priests.

Back in Calgary, our family started to go to a nice Lutheran church that was close by. They were pretty middle-of-the-road Christians, and explained to me that *elders* actually meant *older men*. The Mormons couldn't even get that right. The Lutheran church was a good start for normal, or orthodox, Christianity. My sons and I got baptized by sprinkling; Katie had been baptized as a baby.

In 1990, I quit my job at Field Aviation over a payroll dispute. My new boss was from the military and we didn't see eye to eye. He had replaced the Chief, whom I liked, and who was demoted. I did some electrical work at a construction site in the meantime.

By 1991, Katie suggested, after seeing the new house our Lutheran church was building for the new pastor, that I should go into ministry. I really felt called.

The pastors of the Lutheran church were not keen on helping me go into ministry, though, especially if it was not their branch (a Wisconsin, USA denomination). However, a more liberal Lutheran church (Canadian), and its pastor, did help me. He drove me and another guy to a few Bible colleges in Alberta to check them out.

One of the colleges was Prairie Bible Institute, a historically conservative Bible college in Three Hills, just northeast of Calgary. I knew the moment I stepped onto the campus that I wanted to go there. The plan was to attend for two or four years, get a diploma and do official ministry.

Katie and I decided to sell the house and go for it. Jason was to attend kindergarten at the elementary school on campus. The move would not be hard on the boys, as they didn't have many friends in the neighbourhood and mainly played together in our fair-sized back yard. We had gotten them a great swing set, with white legs decorated with blue and red swirls. They also had a solid plastic fort, and loved their yellow Tonka trucks for playing in the dirt and grass.

Jason and Casey were just great kids and I loved them dearly. Sometimes we'd go to the nearby waterpark, which was surrounded by hills and meadows, and sometimes we'd just lay on our backs on the grass and stare up at the clouds — telling each other what the shapes looked like.

I remember getting them Power Rangers dolls one year and they were also into the Teenage Mutant Ninja Turtles. I enjoyed all these things with the kids, and it was like going through a second childhood with them.

I also famously bought the family a Nintendo system one year. I had gone to the store to buy a vacuum cleaner, but returned with the video game system. That was soon forgiven as Katie became as addicted as the boys playing Super Mario. Those were great times, and Katie and I were pretty good parents, despite our flaws.

### *Astro*

One big problem that we had was Astro, the dog I had gotten from the SPCA to help me do security work at a local mall that was being built.

Astro was a beautiful young German Shepherd. He was famous in our house for the way he ran around the kitchen table and barked his head off when Katie made popcorn in the microwave.

Astro spent most of his time in our fenced backyard, which he loved to dig up, and I would take him for a daily neighbourhood walk to a big empty field. For work, Astro and I would drive to the mall, a couple of kilometres away, a few times at night and on the weekends. We would sometimes wait in the small planning building and do another round before going home.

Now, I had to make a tough decision because of our move: either return Astro to the SPCA, with the chance he would be put down, or I could take him out of town to a field and let him go free. Maybe it was wrong, but I decided to let him go. I prayed about it.

One day, I took him out of town and we walked around a big country field. I said good-bye to him, quickly walked back to the car, hopped in and took off. Astro ran after the car. I could see him in the side mirror. I sped up. Eventually, he was gone. I felt really bad about the situation and prayed for him.

A few days later, shortly before we left, I got a call. An older gent asked me if I was missing a dog. The SPCA had given him our number, based on the tag in Astro's ear. I told him the story. He let me know that Astro had come to his farm and made friends with his other dogs, and that Astro loved to sit with him in his tractor while he farmed. I couldn't believe it. What an answer to prayer! What a great relief to know that Astro would be taken care of and loved. It was great news to share with the family.

## What is Truth?

We sold the house, but Katie was not happy about the selling price as we didn't make any profit. We had stepped out in faith, though, and the student loan to start school came in the week before we left.

When we were all packed up and ready to go, the car sprung a radiator leak, smoke billowing out from under the hood. We bought a bottle of repair fluid, prayed and poured it in. It immediately worked! As soon as it plugged the hole (and the smoke stopped), we jumped in and left.

The car just made it to Prairie, about one kilometre away, and died. But we were happy we had arrived.

# 14

## *Prairie*

Prairie Bible Institute was part of the small Alberta town of Three Hills, 130 kilometres northeast of Calgary. When I attended, Prairie had about five hundred students and the town about three thousand people. Three Hills was a farming community at the foot of three rather large hills. The campus and the town were quiet. A person could relax and think out there. It was *peaceful.*

The sprawling campus was filled with buildings old and new, which included an administration office, book and music store, small theatre, school buildings, a brand-new gymnasium (being built), dorms and living quarters. There were also elementary and high schools, as more and more married families were attending. There was even a vegetable garden for the students. Everything on the campus, and most things in the town, were within walking distance.

Most of the students were eighteen to twenty-two years old, taking four-year-long courses to go into ministry.

While I attended there were about ten other thirty-somethings, mostly with wives and children – as part of our first-year class. If the wives had the time, they could come to class also, for free. Prairie had been founded in the early 1900s as a conservative Christian college, but was in the middle of big changes.

Prairie was great for a brand-new Christian like me, who had no background in the world-wide or local church. For the first time I heard terms like 'being saved' or 'accepting Jesus as your Lord and Saviour'. Concepts I had never really thought about, although I believed in Jesus and the Bible. The longer I went to the college, the more I learned about church history and denominations. What about the Catholic church, for example? What about the Reformation and all the denominations? Who was right, who was wrong, and what did it all mean? I had a lot to learn.

Ma once told me that when she grew up in New Waterford, Protestants and Catholics walked down different sides of the street. We were officially Protestant and went to Calvin United Church occasionally while living in Low Point, but as you have seen, there was no true Christianity in our house growing up at all, or in our neighbours' homes, who were Catholic.

Katie and the kids settled quickly. We rented an older townhouse on the campus and a first-year student named Jason lived in a room in our basement. We had brought the swing set, Nintendo system and the video games, so they were happy.

# Prairie

Katie loved playing those games as much as the kids. Jason began kindergarten and we walked him to school each day.

My various classes consisted of New Testament studies and there were lots of discussions. I loved it. It was structured but free.

The music class, lead by a husband and wife team, even had great theological discussions. I also loved studying in the library and researching the original Greek words of the New Testament.

I loved one class in particular, where the teacher was Mister Tatlock, an American around fifty-five years old. I think he was a Baptist. In many of his classes, his teaching would turn into preaching and we loved it. He really had some fire to him, in a good balanced way. One day, he talked about the Antichrist, and asked who could it be? He threw up a bunch of pictures on the overhead: Gorbachev, the Pope, Reagan and others. It was an interesting and fun discussion.

In one of his classes, after I answered a question, Mr. Tatlock said, 'We need to give you some preaching time, brother.' I felt good about that.

In the middle of the school week, we had a wonderful thing called Chapel, held in the big old Tabernacle Church. We heard different speakers each week, who were accompanied by a praise and worship band, consisting of three or four people, lead by a female and a male singer.

This was a new and incredible experience for me. This was the first time I heard many popular Christian songs.

# CAPE BRETON ORPHAN

The humble band was great, and the worship music was real and uplifting.

Prairie was big into sports. With the freshmen (first-year students), I played floor hockey and flag football. Two incidents showed me that God was working on my character. During one floor hockey game, in the old gym, a small guy ran me from behind and smashed me into the wall. It was a good thing I got my arms up to protect myself. There was supposed to be no checking.

I was instantly mad and plotted my revenge. At the right time, I dropped him to the ground with a hard check. Everyone from both teams raced over and got between us. I would have fought him, but he wasn't interested. Both of us got sent off. We returned later in the game with no further issues.

Another time, while playing flag football, the older students were hammering our first-year guys. There was supposed to be no tackling, only blocking. One fair-sized player mowed down our guys on every offensive play. Again, it made me angry, and I waited.

After a play, when he had his guard down, I nailed him with a hard 'block' and down he went. He jumped up quickly, cocked his fist and mumbled something about brotherly love. I was ready to go, but nothing further happened. When I went to the sideline, our coach (another music teacher), commended me for my 'toughness.' I was surprised by his reaction and my new-found courage.

As an outsider, I saw some things that I didn't like at Prairie. For example, during a big youth event at campus, designed to recruit youth from North America, the leaders put on various activities. Classes were suspended during these days. Parts of the campus transformed into a circus. Inside the hallowed Tabernacle, the youth leaders constructed a wrestling ring, and just like the World Wrestling Federation (now WWE), they performed matches.

There were two teams: Jesus and the good guys versus the devil and the bad guys — youth leaders and students wrestling in the ring. It was cringe-worthy. They even made wrestling cards of the stars — like baseball or hockey cards. I thought it was ludicrous and disrespectful.

There were some activities for the youth, like wall-climbing in the gym, that I thought were perfectly fine.

The youth leaders also brought in Christian rock bands to play in the Tabernacle, at night time. This made some of the older Christians living in the town very angry. I saw and heard an older gent rebuking one of the youth leaders. The bands played sort of heavy rock music accompanied by fog and a light show, the members wearing sunglasses. A bunch of the female and male students joined them on stage to rock on. As someone who just got saved from this whole partying scene, I had to agree with the old men. What the heck was this stuff doing inside the church?

I still remember the poster for the youth event: *Kicking the Doors Out*, with the illustration of church doors being kicked out. Yes, that's exactly what they were doing. But was it good? Some of these youth leaders, men in their thirties and forties, didn't seem like solid Christians at all.

Another thing I disliked was the church's love for a book series called *The Lion, the Witch and the Wardrobe* by C.S. Lewis. Prairie hosted a cinema night, once a week at the gym, and showed videos based on the book. Many families with young kids attended. Lewis was highly lauded by the Christians as a great intellectual and author. But I was bothered by the magic elements in the story and wondered if this was something that Christians should be watching or reading.

Another thing I noticed, associated with C.S. Lewis and other intellectuals, was that the church loved higher education. Just get 'Dr.' in front of your name and you were a great authority and could command a high salary. However, I learned that high-mindedness was actually harming the church more than helping. Jesus was *not* highly educated. And even in his lifetime, this fact confounded the religious leaders. How did Jesus get such great wisdom, they thought, without studying at their schools? They didn't realize that wisdom is a gift that comes from God.

Most classes at Prairie ended with a prayer time. In one class, they prayed for someone to lead a high school Bible study. When no one volunteered, I finally did. Someone then gave me the address of the house on campus where it was held and told me a little about the students. I decided to teach them the Book of Romans. I did a little research on Roman life in the first century, which was incredibly interesting, and went to the first night.

Twelve students attended. The young people enjoyed

the Bible study and seemed very interested. We had excellent discussion. We continued on for a month, one night a week. Then, another teacher showed up, whom I guess the mom, in whose house we were meeting, must have invited. They took a turn leading, and started to play 'camp games' as if it was summer at a Christian camp. So, after one or two weeks of that, I stopped going.

Shortly thereafter, I met one of the students, Desiree, in line at the Oasis lounge — a place for students and teachers to relax, have a coffee and chit chat. She asked me why I had stopped coming. I asked her if she wanted the truth. She said, 'Yes.' I told her that Bible study should really be about studying, and not just playing games.

She replied that the students had enjoyed my Bible studies. She was obviously unhappy that I had stopped coming. It made me happy and sad at the same time. I was happy for the confirmation of what I thought, and sad that I had stopped going. In hindsight, I should have stood my ground for the students and asked them what they wanted.

I met a wonderful older student at Prairie named Gord, and his sweet wife, Joyce. They were in their fifties and lived in the married quarters. Gord was a bit of a rebel, like me, asking the teachers some tough questions. We both liked the old King James Bible, which was a great bond. Some nights after supper, I would go to their house for an hour or two and we would talk about God and life. Of course, we had coffee and cake too! The next thing you know it would be around midnight. Those were great times of fellowship.

Gord was sort of Pentecostal, and had a friend named Larry, who visited him and Joyce at Prairie. This friend was what I would call *extreme* Pentecostal — believing in all kinds of healings, tongues, and miracles. Although I thought that miracles were possible, I was convinced that most were fake. Gord told me that Larry, also in his fifties, would tell fantastic tales about how giant angels would appear behind him in a dangerous situation and scare off bad guys who wanted to harm him. Stories like that.

I discussed these issues with Gord, and he would question Larry. Over time, Gord believed in wild Pentecostalism less and less. One thing I appreciate about Pentecostals, though, is that they want something more than just hum-drum boring Christian rituals. They want a living relationship with God. And what I like about Baptists, is their emphasis on the Word of God. The truth seemed to be in the middle.

During our time at Prairie, we found out that Katie was pregnant. Soon, a beautiful little girl would be on the way. Christina.

We spent Christmas on the campus in our old townhouse. The college was quiet, as the school was closed, and a blanket of snow covered everything. Alcohol was outlawed at Prairie, so, one day, I snuck to the town liquor store and back, buying beer for Katie and me.

Once the Spring session started up, I increasingly questioned my teachers. Their end-time philosophies put them at odds with mainstream Protestants like Anglicans, Lutherans and Presbyterians.

Later, I would find out that this belief system is called Dispensationalism, and focuses on 'end-time prophesy' (think the *Left Behind* series of books and movies). I started to argue with one teacher in particular, and one day he stopped answering my questions, so I packed up my books and papers and walked out of the class. Never to return.

Prairie was really not what I thought it would be. It was not a seminary and was focused on the wrong things.

So, it was April, 1992, almost one full (school) year in, and I decided to quit. Katie supported me and back to Calgary we went. In hindsight, maybe I should have stayed and obtained a diploma. I don't think that I was a good husband or father at this time, and was too focused on my own ambitions.

However, I also think that with Prairie's end time theories — and that subject dominating all their other views — it would not have ended well in any case.

Back in Calgary, we rented a small house and went back to a somewhat normal life. But we were struggling financially and wondering what our future held. Katie gave birth to Christina in August. She was now 3 for 3 with C-sections and brown-eyed children.

I had learned about a small denomination while at Prairie called the Sunday School Mission and they were looking for pastors. They had a vacancy in Deadwood, very far north of Edmonton.

By that September we were sitting in Deadwood and ready for our first crack at ministry.

# 15

## *Deadwood*

I met with the leaders of the Sunday School Mission and they approved me for the posting. They also travelled to Deadwood shortly after we arrived and did an ordination service to install me as the pastor of the small church.

One night before we left, I had a dream, and in the dream the kids and I walked down an old west road, and a bunch of cowboys walked down the same road in the opposite direction.

Once again, as we were all packed up and ready to drive with our trailer attached, there was a problem with the car.

This was the car that Jason (the teen who stayed with us at Prairie) and his family had bought us. It was leaking radiator fluid. But, fortunately, I was able to do a quick repair on a hose and off we went.

It was late August, and after a very long drive (approximately ten hours), we arrived at night.

Some fellow in Peace River, who gave us directions for Deadwood, sent us on the wrong road, a back road, but at least we got to see how isolated these farming communities were. We would spot house lights here and there as it got darker. Deadwood was a very small farming community (by population), with houses spread out kilometers from each other. It was officially a hamlet.

As we pulled up to the address in Deadwood, we saw that the church had provided us with an old single mobile home with an attachment for us to live in. On the first night there a couple of people met us in the gravel parking lot. They decided that the mobile home still needed some work, so we were to stay at a member's home for a day or two. The next day we got to check out the inside of the mobile home and see the old church building.

The stone church building was decayed with cracks in the foundation — and that was very symbolic of their church. The physical church hadn't been used in many years. An old, cantankerous man, Ralph, was the lone elder. He seemed to be of German background with a stern face. Later, I would find out that Ralph had been 'a thorn in the flesh' to the last young pastor also.

At the beginning, there were about twenty-five or so people at this church; maybe thirty on a good Sunday. At my ordination service, we had a lot of visitors, and the possibilities seemed better.

The church services were held in the Deadwood community hall, which meant transforming a room into a church and setting up chairs, etc. The church also gave us a strange mini-washer for the mobile home that we had to hook up at the kitchen sink — for washing clothes.

But we were thankful for all that we had and ministry began. There was also a small post office not far from us. The whole feel of our new situation was like *Little House on the Prairie*.

There were some very nice folks at this church, but there were a few bad apples whose focus was on the wrong things. One of my first messages was on the crack in the foundation of the physical church building, which was a picture for this church. I explained what a spiritual foundation should be. They didn't like that too much. Another time I suggested we collect money and send it to an international charity for a crisis that was happening at the time. After church, they admonished me for not clearing that with them first.

Another sore spot with some members in the church: I wanted to spend some of the money laying around in the bank account (about $18,000!) to help one of our families — by painting their old, decrepit house. The leaders were against that also. They seemed to be against everything, really. No wonder that they had gone through many pastors through the years. The country folk sure didn't like this city slicker coming in and trying to change things up.

I also realized that they hadn't had elections in a while (according to their own constitution), and decided to have an election for the elders. At this point it was only Ralph. When he didn't get 100% support he wanted to quit. We convinced him to stay, for now. I also suggested that we should have more than one elder. I think Ralph saw me as someone trying to undermine his authority.

I also began a floor hockey and Bible study event for Friday nights. It was well received and the amount of kids and teens seemed to go up each week. I loved both parts of it.

The mobile home we lived in was surrounded at the base by hay stacks for insulation. The snow started to fall in September and stayed. The days got colder and shorter, fast! Winters were extreme up there. It was normal to be at minus twenty to minus thirty, and once in a while we hit minus fifty! Cars have to be plugged in and you have to be stocked up on supplies.

The snow stays until April or May. The locals don't put a 'negative' in front of the low temperatures when talking about it. They just say it's twenty-five, when they actually mean minus twenty-five.

The countryside was quite beautiful and peaceful. We were surrounded by farm fields in all directions. Whenever I tell people about *Deadwood*, and mention the name, they chuckle. It actually came from a man who moved there from Deadwood, South Dakota.

I started to visit families in the community and invite them to church and check on them — to see if they had any needs. I also took our regular turn visiting patients at the hospital in the town of Manning. Our church also took a turn, once per month, to minister to the old folk's home in Manning, which consisted of a short sermon and lots of singing. The seniors loved it and so did our little church.

One of the Deadwood families (the Ashworths) needed some help on their farm, so I got to drive a tractor for harvest season, and also got to feed their large pigs while they were away one time. I had to go very early in the morning to feed them. The first time I went in, it was a bit scary as all the pigs crush against your legs trying to get the food. You have to throw the feed to the side to get them away from you. But it was a great experience to meet all the farm animals and to be a farmer, even if briefly. They paid me for the work I did.

Ulla was a wonderful lady who attended our church with her son, Chauncey. Her husband, Ken, was a really nice guy, but was an atheist and did not attend. We prayed for him a lot. That year he had to get cancer treatments and he thanked us for praying for him. It's really amazing sometimes to watch God at work.

Katie had her hands full with the house and kids, and that funny washer. We got the boys plugged into their new school and they took the bus each day. However, the writing was on the wall in regards to the Deadwood church. I learned that this particular church had gone through a series of pastors over the years. The longer we stayed, the more I was questioned. Over the weeks, the numbers dwindled, and we only had a few families still sticking with us by the end.

On some nights, as we got deeper into winter, we heard a scratching sound in our bedroom closet area. We had a mouse trap in the house and had caught a couple already.

One night, while I was lying on the couch, Katie walked out from the bedroom, crying and saying that something just bit her hand in bed!

She had a small puncture wound with blood on her finger. We made sure that Christina was safe and couldn't find the mouse, or rat. It must have disappeared back to where it came from.

We stayed at Barb's house in Manning for a few days. She and her kids attended our church. Her son played video games, and though a bit older, he hit it off with the boys. Some people told us about potential housing in Manning.

Manning was a town of about 1,500 people — about thirty kilometres to the north. The town was divided in the middle by the main highway and had the Notikewan river running through and around it. Manning had all the normal amenities of life — including two schools, various churches, a bank, two grocery stores, and a hockey rink. It was a vibrant town and I really liked it!

We ended up renting a nice modern duplex on the northwest side of town. So, in a short period of time, I quit the Deadwood church, and we moved to Manning and started our own church — Faith Baptist Church. We ended up getting a loose affiliation with a Peace River Baptist church (the denominational head office was in Calgary).

For church, we rented a building in Manning which was mainly for the Elks Lodge, one of those men's groups. The building had a few spacious rooms and a large kitchen. The kitchen was great for our potluck meals, which we had often. (Those wonderful potluck meals showed the closeness of our small church).

The building was used for wedding receptions a lot, and I got the joy of cleaning cigarettes, ashtrays and left-over alcoholic drinks — a reminder of Ma's drinking nights — before church started, on more than one occasion.

In the room that we used for church, I would pull down the antlers plaque off the wall and hang our nice solid wooden cross. I would then put out all the chairs and sometimes our little communion table with the crackers and wine (grape juice). The piano player (Vivian) would sometimes show up early to pick out and practice a couple of hymns. We had bought a new keyboard with the money that Vivian and her husband, Marcel, gave to the church. I always prayed by myself before church, hoping for new people to come out each week.

Shortly before Christmas '92, right after the rat episode, Katie and the kids went to Victoria to visit her family. While she was away, the Manning Health Authority phoned and told me that she needed to get a tetanus shot. So Katie did. I'm sure that the story must have spread like wildfire around Deadwood and Manning:

PASTOR'S WIFE BITTEN BY RAT!

# 16

## *Manning*

After the family returned in January '93, Katie surprised me with a bottle of Asbach, which we enjoyed on different nights. The drinking, as well as my occasional smoking, was done in secret. I was still in the Prairie mindset where alcohol was not allowed (officially).

Life returned to somewhat normal in '93. We became very good friends with an older First Nations couple who lived in the other half of the duplex. John and Josephine were already Christians and joined our church. They also came over for Wednesday night Bible studies. Eventually, Josephine's sister and her husband joined us too. Sometimes, we would have about 15 people at our home for Bible study. The study, with questions and discussion, made for some great evenings, and the fellowship always included coffee and cake.

I really liked Manning. In winter, you could watch the spectacular northern lights dance across the sky and enjoy the small-town Christmas feel as the stores and houses displayed their seasonal lights. In the summers, it seemed like the sun never went down. I played slow pitch baseball with a local team, and Katie and the kids loved coming out to the games and socializing with the other women (some who played on the team) and other kids. We made friends with some of the players — one time playing board games at a player's house.

I also worked at the local IGA grocery store to make ends meet. I was a cashier mostly. The new church was still pretty small (about 20 people) and could not pay much, but we had everything we needed, and the kids always had nice clothes and good food.

One good ministry I accomplished in Manning was working on the *Jesus* film project in '93. The video is a straight-up, humble film about his life.

We held a big community breakfast where many in the town came out to have a breakfast and donate to the cause. The money raised would purchase *Jesus* videos — one for each house in the town. This project had already been repeated many times throughout North America and the world, and I was made the official Manning coordinator.

We worked with the Catholic church to get the project done. The two Pentecostal churches refused to work with me on this project. I was the new pastor in town and guess they wanted me to have their approval. The younger pastor, close to my age, said that I shouldn't come into town with guns ablaze — something like that. That was pretty rich coming from them, seeing how their Pentecostal church was split into two in such a small town.

Despite the outward appearance of a young pastor and his family doing good ministry in the community, things were not great at home. Katie and I were growing apart. Looking back, as I said before, I should have made Katie and the kids a bigger priority in my life. Katie and I were comfortable in a way, but not deeply loving towards each other. We did, however, love the kids.

For her first birthday, I remember we got Christina a special cake made up from someone in town and us blowing out the candle at the table.

For Christmas '93, I got the boys a red metal hockey net and all of us sticks and a road hockey ball. We played out on the snow-covered road in front of our house. It was a blast. I also got to go to the rink and help the kids learn to skate with the elementary school.

In summer, I taught the boys how to catch with gloves and a ball, and play some base runner games in the back yard (what we called hot dog). The boys also made friends with a couple of other children from a house behind us, and they would catch and play with frogs in a small pond of water behind the house. More than once, we had to holler for the kids to come along for church.

While I think I was doing some things right for the ministry, I still had a large character flaw not fully dealt with: my eye for good-looking women. I also had developed some pride (not a good thing) in how I looked. One woman from our church, when introducing me to another woman one day on a sidewalk in Manning, said, 'Too bad they don't all look like this, eh?'

Something along those lines. For someone who had been an ugly duckling, those comments went to my head a bit.

In February '94, Katie told me she wanted to separate and go back to Victoria. I agreed, thinking some time apart would do us good. She got the kids' school transfer all arranged. On the day of the departure, I drove Katie and the kids to the bus terminal in Grande Prairie. I cried on the way back as the reality of the situation sank in. Was I losing my family? This was a big eye opener for me. I did a lot of praying and thinking in the next couple of months. Katie and I had some calls over that time, and she made it clear she was not coming back. I remember one heated phone call when she told me that.

One night I had a dream, and in the dream Katie and I were picking some big grapes. I was gathering mine into a basket (or some container). However, Katie was getting drunk on her grapes. I tried to tell her that what she was doing was wrong.

In April, about two months after they left, I drove to Victoria. When I arrived at Ed's house, where Katie and the children were living, I was shocked to see that Katie had transformed back to *Party Katie* — the teen I had met in Germany. *Pastor's Wife Kati*e was gone. Her father had bought her a car, and Katie was going out a lot to dances and parties.

I stayed at the house while I was down and Ed and Sheila went away for a few days. Some of Katie's old friends (from her school days) dropped by the house.

I already knew some of them from my first visit to Victoria. They were in party mode and still getting drunk a lot. One of her male friends threw up at the kitchen table. It was unreal.

When I first came down, after checking in with Katie and Christina (who was sleeping), I went to Ruth King Elementary School to surprise the boys. I stood by the chain-link fence about fifty feet away from the entrance. As all the kids poured out of the school, I spotted Jason and then Casey tagging behind. Jason saw me.

"It's Dad!" he hollered to Casey and they both came running. What a great moment that was: big hugs and kisses.

I stayed in Victoria for a week or so. Katie told me again that she was not coming back to Manning, but that I could move down and see what happens. A day or two before I left, there was a knock at the front door and someone said it was for me. I answered and a guy handed me some documents. It was court papers. Katie had filed for custody and support money (and possibly divorce). I went to the basement, sat down in a chair and read the docs. It was all pretty shocking. Ed came down to check on me, as he knew some serious things were happening.

The morning I left to go back to Manning, Jason hugged me hard and cried. I felt so bad. But I knew I was coming right back for good. I would just go back, sell some things, pack the rest and move to Victoria. I knew I had to be there for the kids. I would be back soon. And if that's what happened, it would have been just fine.

But I took a short detour before I returned to Victoria — a short and catastrophic one.

# 17

## *Detour*

I drove back to Manning, informed the church members that I was moving to Victoria, and that was it. The members agreed with my decision. I put up some signs around town for a moving sale and proceeded to sell most items. Lots of people started to drop by the house. One woman in particular dropped by with her mother-in-law. Her name was Ella and she had recently come to our small church a couple of times; accompanied by an older woman from our church. Ella was about my age, had lately come from South Africa, and just married a local farmer (who didn't attend our church). She openly told me she was already separating from her husband and asked how to rent my place.

Ella was pretty with light brown hair. We talked a bit and exchanged phone numbers.

After she left, we began phoning each other, and one day we agreed to meet. I picked her up, and she came to my place for the afternoon.

Ella and I expressed our affection for each other and, after she returned to her house, our phone calls picked up again.

We made a secret plan to leave town together and go to my sister's place in St. Paul, close to Edmonton.

I really felt like a sneak at this time. Ella would hide if anyone came to the house when she was there, or when she was in the car. I was not upfront with the members of the church as I left town. This whole development was sudden and bad.

When I left town a few days later, Ella left with me. It was a colossal error. Of course, I justified this to myself in every way possible, but even the optics were bad. It may have looked like we had an affair while I was the pastor, or it was the reason that Katie left. But neither scenario was true. It all happened in a very short period of time. And, as soon as it began, it was over.

We stayed together at Alison's house for about a month and then moved out into our own apartment. But very quickly, Ella patched things up with her husband and I was the odd man out. She also seemed to have an eye for other men, even while she was with me. She told me that she liked to flirt and had done so for a long time. In hindsight, it seems that this was all some kind of sport for her.

In spiritual terms, this was a spiritual attack. This whole episode was meant to destroy my ministry, my name and me. I was really struggling emotionally at this time. I had now been dumped twice, in quick succession.

The old lonely orphan feelings returned and I headed back to Victoria.

Looking back, I'm glad this relationship ended as fast as it did. However, it was a sting that would last a long time. I found out later that even on her bus ride back to the Manning area, she met another guy who started to contact her. And even though her husband and neighbour (the woman from our church) tried to work on her — Ella was impossible — and her husband finally kicked her out and back to South Africa. *Good riddance*!

This was an extremely painful lesson for me. I had rushed in and given my heart way too quickly (again!). But it would not be the last time. I still had one more gigantic blunder to go through before God would finally get through to me on this vital issue.

# 18
## *Victoria*

After that detour, I finally made it back to Victoria and concentrated on getting my life back on track and focusing on the kids. At first, I stayed at Katie's parent's house, where I spent tons of time with the kids and often took them to the park. Her house was actually in a suburb called Langford, which was about a twenty-minute drive to downtown Victoria.

Katie continued to party and go to rock concerts. I made a plan to sell the car and enroll in a small business college in downtown Victoria.

Selling the car, a black Monte Carlo, was an ordeal, as it looked and ran great — but would not go into reverse! I finally had to get the transmission fixed to sell it. The car had been a generous gift from a church member in Manning.

I rented a small room in a house close to the ocean, and it was within walking distance to the college. The four-month long course was Micro Computer Business

Applications, focusing on programs like Word and Excel, typing, bookkeeping and office administration. It ran from September to December and I really enjoyed it. It was a brand-new world for me.

The house I lived in turned out to be a major Buddhist house, where people came to chant and meditate. That was another story, which would fill a chapter.

During my time at the business college I also worked at a local grocery store which provided essential income. Katie moved a couple of times during this period. This would begin a long stretch of trying to keep up with Katie and her many moves with the kids.

I got the children every second weekend. We'd go to the local children's park on Cook Street, beside Beacon Hill Park, which was all close to my place. It was a great little park. We had tons of fun there over the years. It had swings, a fair size field, and a wooden obstacle course raised off the ground — where I would chase the kids from the ground, in a tag type game. We also played some football games, with Jason and Casey taking turns as the receiver or defender. I was the quarterback, and Christina, who was much younger than the boys, was the hiker.

I graduated from the business college shortly before Christmas. Katie had a new boyfriend (Bill) by this time, whom she would end up marrying. I actually babysat the children at Katie's new apartment in Langford a few times when she went out to party. I saw more and more partiers coming to the house where she lived, and more and more men who I didn't know.

I had started to attend a Lutheran church in Victoria. Despite the setbacks, I was still growing.

I only occasionally drank and smoked — and tried to quit smoking for good.

During this time, a beautiful young blonde woman at the Lutheran church hit on me. This was certainly a test, and I was glad that I could see it. I thought and prayed about it. She was engaged and didn't seem to care much about her fiancé, who was always tagging along behind her. She was very friendly to me at church, and one day said that she had wanted to call me the night before. *Warning bells*! I ended up giving her the cold shoulder, which was my first real victory in this area. I felt really good about my actions.

In the first half of '95, I searched for employment in bookkeeping or office work, but was unsuccessful. Thankfully, I still worked at the grocery store, although the hours and pay were not enough.

## *Lisa*

I moved a couple of times over the next months, and now lived in a very nice condo, roommate of a guy who I did not know but who just needed someone to help with the rent. This was just up the road from the park on Cook Street. I was glad to be back to this area, which I loved and was close to everything I loved — like the ocean, park, work and church.

In the summer of '95, at the Lutheran church, I met Lisa, a short red-haired girl.

She was pretty with blue eyes and freckles and always seemed to sit by herself in a pew. One Sunday at church, they gave out cards and the pastor asked us to invite someone to something.

After church, I found Lisa sitting outside in her brother's car, talking away with him. I stopped beside the car, bent down, handed my card to Lisa and invited her out for lunch. She quickly said good-bye to her brother and hopped out. She accepted and we had lunch at my apartment. I made us tomato soup with crackers and bread. *The last of the great chefs*!

Over the next month or so, we went out on a few more dates; mostly watching videos at each other's places. I visited her at her small cottage house, which was white with blue trim, on the other side of Beacon Hill Park. Her area of town was called James Bay. She and her mother, Selma, had a business of buying, renovating and selling houses, so I helped Lisa with chores surrounding that. We would clean up, mow the grass and hang up signs in the area for the open house — as they wanted to sell the house themselves. Selma just happened to be away on vacation for this first month of our relationship, and it was no coincidence that it was our happiest time together.

One night, after watching a movie together at Lisa's house, I spent the night. We began living together after that. Once again, I rushed in. As I look back, I understand why they had courting in the older days.

As the days unfolded, I realized that there were some strange things in Lisa's house. She had a gold Buddha in her closet and a strange book that came with some weird bones, which she threw one night to see what they said about our relationship. I realized that this was some kind of witchcraft and told her she should not be using those kinds of things. She told me that her mother had given them to her. I would realize over time, that Selma was what we call New Age, meaning that she could hold all sorts of beliefs at the same time — for example Christianity and witchcraft and other religions — like Buddhism.

I should have known that just because a person attends church does not make them a Christian. And being a Christian, and trying to actually live it, was now the most important thing in my life. So, this was not a small matter to me.

It dawned on me that Lisa was not really 'born again'. Her family had attended the Lutheran church as a family tradition for many years, but had no close personal relationship with Jesus. Lisa was getting baptized at the church in the near future, so I tried to teach her as much as I could.

One time, during that first summer together, we had to go check on Selma's and her husband's house in Lake Cowichan while they were away. They lived right beside the river and were both artists. Lisa took us swimming, with masks, snorkels, and flippers across the fast-moving and dangerous Cowichan river.

It was a wondrous experience. We swam from one side to the other and viewed the salmon swimming upstream, and bubbles rising from the clams below.

Lisa also introduced me to classical music at this time, which I loved. I was especially drawn to the music of Pachelbel, which we ended up playing at our wedding.

When Selma returned from vacation, she had us up to meet me and we visited her and her husband many times over the next few months. Selma checked me out during these visits. As in all new relationships it all went rather smoothly at the start. But over time, everyone's true character started to emerge. Selma was *ever-present* in our lives, and mother and daughter were joined at the hip.

Selma was also short and fancied herself some kind of life teacher. She followed various New Age teachers — listening to their tapes and buying their books. I found that most of what she tried to teach Lisa was pretty shallow, with no real substance.

One day, back in Victoria, Lisa asked me to marry her. I said, 'Yes,' but told her it was my duty to ask her. So, I asked her shortly thereafter. We picked out wedding rings and an engagement ring and started to plan the wedding. We also had to make sure we were both officially divorced. Her previous marriage was also over by about a year.

One time, while we met with my lawyer, Lisa became agitated, raised her voice and shouted at him for moving too slow on my divorce. It was a shocking embarrassing outburst, and another warning sign that I should have been paying attention too.

Selma often invited us up to Lake Cowichan to work on her house and property. She paid us, which was very helpful.

One time, while scrubbing the floor together, she and Lisa had an argument about something. Selma then said, in front of me, that Lisa had a problem with lying, that she thought it had been addressed, but wasn't. Lisa just looked down, kept scrubbing, and didn't say anything in her own defence. I should have taken that warning sign more seriously also.

That night, Lisa and I had an argument about what was said between her and her mom. She got very angry, took off her engagement ring and tossed it away outside in the dark. I found it and gave it back to her. Lisa's anger was often explosive and over the top, and I was just starting to realize it.

But it was too late.

# 19

## *The Bulldozer*

Lisa's mother was a big problem in our marriage and even before. Selma was constantly interfering in every decision we made. Once she even complained to Lisa about how much ice cream we were buying. Over time I would learn that this was all about control over Lisa's life.

One day in September we found out that Lisa was pregnant. We did that little test kit you can buy from the pharmacy. We were extremely happy. We started to work more on our wedding plans, but those plans were soon hijacked by Selma, who quickly got involved.

Over time, the wedding, planned for January, turned into Lisa and Selma's wedding. I would often overhear them making plans. Closer to the wedding, I realized they planned on having a swan theme. *Swans? Where did they get that from?* They were arranging swan napkins, swan this and swan that. I finally spoke up and put an end to the swan craziness.

At the beginning, Lisa wanted to make her own wedding dress, and showed me various patterns she was thinking about. Selma convinced her to buy one, so that they could go shopping for one.

Lisa and I would sometimes talk about her mother, as I tried to open Lisa's eyes about the manipulation. Lisa described Selma to me as a bulldozer who never backed off an issue. That turned out to be a great description. Lisa also told me that her first marriage failed because she and her mother constantly overruled Richard on everything. They drove him so crazy, he had to eventually see a psychiatrist. He eventually left town — never to return.

We finally decided to get married at the Lutheran church and had the reception there also. It was a small traditional wedding. Lisa's family attended, along with my children and friends from the church. Lisa wore a white dress and the boys and I had nice bluish tuxedos. Christina was the flower girl in a nice dress. During the ceremony, the pastor had us both light our candles from the main bigger candle. The sermon was about blueprints and whose blueprint we should follow in marriage. Meaning Lisa's or mine. In hindsight, I think the pastor got that wrong. Lisa argued a lot with her last husband and now me. The blueprint we both needed to be following was God's.

Immediately after the wedding, the bride and groom were supposed to stand outside in the foyer and greet everyone as they congratulated us on our wedding. Lisa quickly disappeared (for a long time) and everyone asked me where she was. She had gone off with her mother and the photographer to get photos of Lisa and her wedding dress. That was another sign for where we were.

At the reception, in a large room in the church basement, Selma sat at the head table and showed off her latest art — a large round carving of swans that was meant to depict Lisa, me and the children. I remember the pastor giving her a disapproving look as he and I had talked privately about Selma.

For the honeymoon, we went to an upscale hotel close to the inner harbour. It was beautiful. A year later, I booked the same hotel for a surprise anniversary present for Lisa, but she refused to go in because she wasn't dressed for it. I had to turn the car around and go home and wait for Lisa to dress for the occasion. The Caper in me thought that was prideful of her.

I was really bothered that Lisa couldn't be happy and spontaneous in these surprise situations. To me, a person should accept these acts of love with joy and gratitude.

*But not Lisa.*

For Christmas '96, I bought her a very nice winter coat, but she rejected it and even said that her mother knew her tastes better. I guess the writing was on the wall.

Al and Phyllis were Lisa's father and stepmother. Phyllis had been working at the dental clinic owned by Al and family.

When Al and Selma broke up, Al and Phyllis began dating, and they were now married. Phyllis, who was much younger than Al, was very nice to my children and me.

And even though she was now wealthy, I think she came from a hard-working family and therefore had a soft spot for us. I remember her getting clothes for the children and starting me off on my bookkeeping career at the dental clinic. She taught me how to do the computerized accounting. She also started a bank account for each of the children and put a little in each month.

I didn't know it when I first met her, but Phyllis had cancer — it had been in remission, however it had now returned. She used to cover one eye with her hand when showing me things on the computer screen because the cancer had spread to her eye. I wanted to witness to Phyllis as she became sicker and ended up in the hospital and also when she was brought home, but Lisa and Selma made a big effort to block me.

At the same time, Selma was trying to be Phyllis's best friend and tried to convince her that Phyllis would be an angel and watch over her son after she died. It was New Age fairy tales.

Selma had such a poor feel for interfering that when Phyllis's mother came to see her at the hospital, she demanded that Selma stay away from Phyllis.

I was at the house when Phyllis passed away, and I could feel something the moment she died.

## *The Ministry of Health*

My work at the dental clinic helped me land a full-time job with the Ministry of Health as an administrative clerk working on service seniority.

## The Bulldozer

The job entailed going through physical files and adding and checking each person's total union seniority. It was an excellent office job with very good pay.

In June of '96, I started my new job at the Ministry and Hayley was born the same month. I was there in the delivery room for yet another C-section. Mom and baby were perfectly fine.

Two issues came up with Selma during the birth. First, she was ever present and I could tell she wanted to be in the delivery room at birth. (I think she wanted to take photos or a video). Lisa's doctor asked me if I wanted anything before she did the C-section, and I said, 'Yes, please make sure Selma is not in the room during the birth.' She did, and I'm sure Selma held that against me.

After the birth of Hayley, who was beautiful with blue eyes and blonde hair, I held her for a bit then I gave her back to Lisa and left the room to go and phone everyone — the dad's joyful duty! When I walked down the hall way to use the phone, I ran into Selma, who smiled at me and told me she had already phoned everyone.

In June, '96, I bought the three older kids an inexpensive new dome tent for a grading present. I think it was only forty dollars. The green tent could fit the three of them easily. There were no plans to go camping yet, but it was a great backyard activity. I set it up so they could play in and around it.

Some days later, Lisa informed me that Selma was unhappy that we had spent money on this tent, and that she had a second-hand one to give the kids.

## CAPE BRETON ORPHAN

I couldn't believe it and basically laughed it off.

One morning, I woke up with a big orange tarp thing all rolled up and sitting beside my side of the bed with a letter resting on it. At first, I didn't know what the orange blob was. I read the letter. It was all about how I should accept Selma's second hand tent and return the new one I had bought for the children. It was unreal. I'm sure that Lisa was lying there, facing away from me, with her eyes wide open as this all unfolded. We argued about the tent throughout the day.

Selma phoned later that day to make sure that all was okay. Lisa was positive and thankful to her mother on the phone and assured her that it did not cause any problems — which was a bold-faced lie. I stood right beside Lisa and the phone. We argued as soon as Lisa hung up.

Lisa exploded and became hysterical, grabbed the large phone off the wall and smashed it to the floor in pieces. She shouted and was freaking out. I put my hand towards her mouth and told her to calm down. She suddenly grabbed my hand and bit into it. I was in pain and shock. Her teeth marks were in my hand. Realizing what she had done, she ran upstairs, crying.

After recovering from the shock, and letting time pass, I climbed up the stairs to our bedroom. Lisa was sobbing, but I couldn't see her.

I went to the door of the small closet that ran down the wall. She was sitting in there in the dark, quite far away, and crying. I asked her what she was doing in there, crawled in and brought her out.

## The Bulldozer

She then examined my hand and repeatedly kissed it, feeling quite bad. I was starting to realize that there was something deeply disturbing going on here.

Other things that Lisa had done during our short time together included grabbing Jason by the front and back of the head when she got into a big argument with him. She actually covered his mouth and he felt like he couldn't breathe. He pushed her back. I heard the loud commotion and arrived in the bedroom just as they broke up. Jason told me what happened and Lisa denied it, so I was forced to believe one of them. I had no reason to disbelieve Jason.

Once we ate supper at the table and the kids didn't like the peas. Lisa got angry and forced Jason to eat them even though he was almost gagging. I flat out told the children in front of her that they didn't have to eat them if they didn't like them. That was probably another nail in the coffin of our marriage. Lisa was very hard in these situations and didn't have much grace.

Another time, after an argument, we were outside and walked towards the back of the driveway. She opened the heavy wooden gate and smashed it closed. After I examined it, I found she had actually bent the iron handle. She was incredibly strong for someone her size.

The strange thing was, that to neighbours and those outside the house, Lisa had a completely different personality. She was the sweetest and nicest person you ever met.

However, it wasn't all bad. Lisa and I did have good times together too.

We walked at the ocean and did lots of family activities in Beacon Hill Park. We also loved attending a dinner theatre up island (a Christmas gift from her mother).

### *The Hayley Miracle*

One day, when Hayley was a few months old, she suddenly became sickly and pale. Lisa was trying to breast feed her at this time, but it wasn't working — not that this was the cause of the sudden illness. We really had no idea what had caused Hayley to become so lethargic. Lisa and I, and Selma, took her to the hospital. The doctor didn't know what was wrong with Hayley, and she seemed to be getting worse. We were worried.

When the doctor and nurse left the room, I told Lisa and her mom what I was about to do. I knelt close to Hayley and intently prayed for her in Jesus' name. I believe that Lisa silently prayed also. Hayley's colour quickly returned, and her condition improved. We left the hospital shortly thereafter.

I believe this was a miracle. Yet, I'm not what you would call wild Pentecostal at all. I think that most Pentecostal healings or the Catholic crying Marys are fake. I just believe that God can heal and do miracles. The Bible says to pray in Jesus's name, and that's simply what we did.

### *Katie Gets Worse*

During my time with Lisa, we were getting the children every second weekend, and I was paying child support. To her credit, Lisa made a nice cover for an air mattress

## The Bulldozer

for the kids and later, with her mother, got them bunk-beds and other necessities.

One time, I drove out to pick up the kids in Langford and Katie met me in the driveway. She was acting weird and offered to sell me her furniture in the basement. I was taken aback and told her I didn't need any.

A month or so later, a woman came to our house while I was at work. She told Lisa that Katie was a severe drug addict and that she was getting many people hooked on drugs around her — and that we should take the kids out of the house. The woman said that her own dad had become an addict because of Katie.

I drove to Child and Family Services in Langford and reported what the lady had told us, but they treated me with disdain — as if I was just an ex looking for revenge. I would face this sexual bias a lot in the future.

On the next trip to Langford, I asked a guy I knew about Katie. Out of earshot of the children, he told me the full bad story. It was all true. Katie was indeed a major drug addict, dragging the kids through hell. She might have been a dealer also.

For the next couple of years, I followed Katie from eviction to eviction, and town to town, up and down the island — trying to stay on top of the children's constantly changing situation. Sometimes I phoned Child and Family Services, and at other times the police.

# 20

## *Big Changes*

I was laid off from the Ministry of Health in April '97. I would get called back towards the end of the year, but it was good timing as baby number two was on the way. Becky was due in August.

When Lisa went into labour, we were all ready and I drove us to the hospital. We argued on the way, which will tell you how bad our relationship was.

Becky was born by C-section. I, or the moms, were now five for five (to use a baseball term). There was a scary couple of minutes when Becky was born as she didn't immediately make a crying sound. It was kind of quiet and hectic as they worked on her — because there was some green stuff surrounding her. But once they got rid of that, she cried and all was well. I was praying for sure! Becky was pretty with red hair and blue eyes.

A month or so after Becky was born, Lisa and I decided to separate. It was a mutual decision. I moved out and took a small apartment nearby — close to the ocean.

## CAPE BRETON ORPHAN

Lisa would drop by on some days on her way to the ocean, and we would walk together, with the girls in the stroller.

Selma and Lisa were making all the decisions about the girls now. Over the coming months, I was pushed out more and more. Lisa kept me in the dark about important issues, including a minor operation that Becky needed in Vancouver. Instead of leaving Hayley in my care, Lisa left her with Selma. I never found out until the last minute and therefore couldn't take care of my own daughter.

I moved back to the house briefly one month, but then rented another apartment further away, close to Bay Street. It was in a bright yellow house, so that's how I always referred to it. I still got the older three kids every second weekend, but without the car it was difficult.

On Fridays, I would walk all the way to Lisa's house, a couple of kilometres away, borrow the car, drive it out to Langford, get the kids and drop them off at the yellow house. Then I would return the car to Lisa and race all the way home again. On Sundays I would repeat the whole car thing in reverse.

The kids and I always had fun on our weekends together. At this time, a woman and her five children lived in another part of the house, and all the kids would run together outside and eat from the plum tree in the back yard.

One day during the week, I dropped by Lisa's and found out that the Ministry of Health had phoned, and I had been recalled to work — doing the same job as before.

## Big Changes

I was *very* happy about that. I would be working in the same building on Blanshard Avenue, very close to the yellow house.

Lisa and I received a bit of marriage counselling at this time, but it wasn't working. I finally gave Lisa an ultimatum and gave her some months to make a decision. I wanted her to leave her mother (and her mother's house) and to move out and make our own life together. After the time had passed, she dropped by the house one day to tell me her decision. She said that she didn't trust me and wanted me to come back and live at the house. I refused.

Work was going well in '98 and I moved into an apartment on Cook Street. It was great as it was walking distance to work, the park and ocean. The older kids were still coming every second weekend, and Lisa brought the girls over once in a while.

By April '98, I had finished the initial work I was hired for. The ministry was going to lay me off again, but Judy, the wonderful supervisor of payroll, kept me on. As they were deciding where I would eventually go, I bounced around a few temporary jobs. I really wanted to get hired permanently in payroll, but they were full at the moment. It is worth noting that most of the staff in this seven-floor building were women. They were dressed to the max every day, and for the guys who worked there it was quite a fashion show, with some flirting mixed in.

In May, I was working on a temporary assignment at Vital Statistics on Fort Street, another building close to the Ministry of Health.

For this job, people phone in and request a birth, death or marriage certificate. We would receive many names on a printed sheet, and then search for their documents on a photo-reader machine. This was a super-fast machine, with knobs that you turned, to scroll through tons of names and documents. We would find the required one and take a photo of it.

One day, while I was working on the photo-reader machine, I suddenly started to get squiggly lines of colour in my vision, towards my right side.

I stood up from my chair and said something like, 'What's going on?' Some colleagues asked me what was happening. I said, 'I don't know, I have these strange colours in my eyes.'

The female boss came over and got me to sit at another desk for a bit. A strong headache ensued (I didn't know it was a migraine at the time) and lasted for quite some time. At one point I got up and looked out the open window, but she suggested I sit down again.

My supervisor and colleagues were concerned. Once things calmed down, about an hour later, I was allowed to go home or to the doctor's. My normal physician, Dr. Yewchuk, happened to be on vacation and the one at the clinic couldn't figure out what had happened to me, just yet.

Over the next few days at work, they tried me at that machine again, but I couldn't work on it. They also tried me on taking calls, but for that job you had to stare at a computer screen to process the orders.

## Big Changes

I often felt weird, and everything seemed brighter than normal, like a glossy magazine. I would find out soon enough that my weird feelings were migraines. I never had anything like that before.

Lisa drove me to one of my medical appointments for a test. They flashed a lot of lights in my eyes, which in hindsight was a real stupid thing to do. I got bad migraines from that, but didn't know what they were yet. Towards evening, I was still at Lisa's house and struggling with lights and feeling weird. Problem was, I still had to walk to my place through Beacon Hill Park, which meant facing car lights and park lamps at night.

As Lisa was getting ready to go out to an event with the girls, she asked me to come upstairs and say good-bye.

I was in the basement with my eyes covered with a cloth and replied something like, 'Dad is sick and can't come up right now.' Lisa then said, loudly, 'Yeah, your dad is sick, all right. Sick in the head.' And then they left. I never forgot that mean statement.

Shortly thereafter, I made the walk home through the streets and the park with every light and lamp bothering me.

I made it home, felt really weird, knelt down on the floor and prayed. I quickly started to feel better and then went in the bedroom and rested my eyes. The biggest issue I had at this time was fear. Fear of not knowing what was going on.

Eventually, Dr. Yewchuck came back to work after being on vacation.

He immediately diagnosed me with photophobia — extreme sensitivity to bright lights — and gave me additional time off work. He was exactly right. I still have the same condition today — but it has plateaued. I had to get and wear sunglasses all the time outside, and whenever I tried to work on a computer. I would sometimes use over-sized sun glasses (like older people wear) or even two pairs — especially in the first couple of years.

My brother Junior told me that his eyes sometimes bothered him and he put crushed ice on his eyelids. Together with other advice, I found the thing that helped me most: lying down in a dark room with a cold wet cloth. After about a half hour of that, my eyes would normally calm down.

When things started to settle down a bit, I went back to work, and finally got a long-term assignment in the Program Funding and Support department — back in the main Blanshard building. This was a great job of ordering and stocking all the office supplies. I worked on the sixth floor with my colleagues. The task also involved talking to all the secretaries of the executives on the seventh floor. I still had to do some computer work and that was a daily struggle. I tried all kinds of glare screens and sunglasses. Even the overhead fluorescent lighting bothered me.

On days when my eyes acted up, I went to the basement of the building, where old equipment was stored. I would let myself in, find a good spot and just stare at the old grey concrete walls with the lights off. It felt so good and calmed my eyes.

I would do that a couple of times a day, or whenever my eyes felt really bad. Overall, I loved my job and worked in a large cubicle area with my more senior colleague, April.

At home, I had to cover the windows with blinds and extra blankets to cut down the sunlight, and I could no longer watch TV. In the first couple of years, I also would occasionally get tiny pings in my vision — little small dots of coloured light — like a pin head of blue. I could no longer drive at night, and that medical fact was eventually put on my driver's licence.

## *A New Roommate*

One day, I got a phone call at work. Katie wanted me to take Jason because she couldn't handle him anymore. He was getting into fights at school and now arguments at home. I was ecstatic about this new development. Jason came to live with me and I got him plugged into Sir James Douglas Elementary School. It was walking distance from where we lived. Jason was twelve years old and made new friends in grade seven quickly.

Jason and I got along great at this time. We would play hockey in the apartment with brooms and a soft ball — each taking turns being the goalie and shooter. I also got him a bike. The new school and principal really supported him. Jason ended up friends with a girl, Zola, who would later turn into his long-time girlfriend. They would sometimes come together to our house for lunch. Jason also had another male friend and would sometimes have a sleep over at his house.

## CAPE BRETON ORPHAN

When Jason first started at his new school, a smart alec pulled his chair out from under him. This was a *big* mistake. Later, in the hallway, Jason met *Mr. Tough Guy* and threw him to the floor. The kid hurt his hand and they called an ambulance.

This could have been a rough start for Jason, but the principal knew his history, talked with me, and gave Jason the grace to keep going. They could have suspended him. I believe that was a big moment in Jason's life and stressed to me how one person, whether a teacher or principal or anyone, could make such a big difference in the life of a child.

No wonder Jason had turned into such a fighter, with all the things going on in his life. Casey, on the other hand, was finding his solace in his Langford school, Ruth King Elementary. His teachers loved him and he excelled, even winning the *Student of the Year* award one year. Christina was doing great in school, and of course, loved her teacher.

One of Casey's teachers, Mr. Green, was a very special person. I went to the school and talked to him a few times. He actually did an affidavit for me in which he described the children coming to school without being properly fed, and their clothes ragged and unclean. That would all play into what was about to happen.

# 21

## *The Image*

In February 1999, something very special happened to me and the kids. For whatever reason, maybe all the turmoil in my life, I was praying for God to show me his love. One evening, out of the blue, there appeared on my bedroom wall a glowing image.

I first started to notice the image at about seven o'clock each evening, as it started to get dark. On the wall opposite the foot of my bed appeared the image of a man on a cross — almost full size. It was vague, but unmistakable, as were the beams making the cross.

You could easily make out a man's head bent down, his long body and a wrapped cloth over his lower area. His body was naked besides that. You could make out his chest and torso down to the cloth. His arm went out along one beam. One side of the cross was more visible than the other. It was as if drawn from a specific angle. The image faded out towards the bottom of his legs. There were no feet or anything lower.

I thought on it and wondered what it meant. This was obviously God's answer to my prayer. I first showed it to Jason, who was now close to thirteen years old. He saw it easily also.

A day or two later, I took the bold step to tell my co-workers, including April Paxton, who shared the cubicle with me. Four or five of them gathered in our cubicle. I didn't know how anyone would respond. After I told them, they were polite, but just left and went back to work. I thought that was the end of it.

Later that day, Cheryl, a woman who worked across from us, and April, asked if they could come to my place to see the image. I agreed. They came one night, and my three older kids were also present. Cheryl had a video camera with her, hoping to film it. We all sat, either on my bed or beside it, waiting. At first there was nothing — which was normal.

After a while, the image started to appear, just like on the other nights. I waited until I could clearly see the image, walked over and —

'I see it,' blurted April, before I had really pointed anything out. But the amazing thing was that it could not be recorded. Cheryl tried, but the camera would not pick it up. The light wasn't strong enough. It was only strong enough for us all to view it. Amazing.

The next day at work, Sylvia, an older supervisor, suggested to us that a person could look at an image on a paper and then see that image when they looked at a wall. But we weren't buying it.

# The Image

April shot that theory down immediately by telling her that she had seen the image. Sylvia had a perplexed look on her face as she quietly left our cubicle.

I also showed the image to a couple of other people on other days, including the landlord's wife, Dorothy. She cried when she saw it and said it restored her faith. I think she had a Catholic background, but was not attending church. The image lasted for about two weeks, and then didn't appear anymore. It was one of the most remarkable things I have ever experienced. Every once in a while when I think about it, it strengthens me. And please remember, I was, and am, a person who is very skeptical about these types of things.

In early March, I was laid off from the Ministry of Health. They knew I was struggling with my eyes, and didn't want me to become a 'regular', and have to pay me any disability. I was closing in on two full years' service, which would have given me full benefits. In hindsight, though, the timing of getting laid off at this time must have come from God, because no one else could know what was about to happen.

Casey and Christina came to stay with us for all of March break. When the break was just about over, Bill, Katie's husband, came to pick up the children.

However, I had seen needles in the back of their car on a previous trip. I went out to the parking lot and told him I was not giving the kids back. He drove away to go tell Katie. It was a big gamble on my part, but it was now or never.

Two Victoria police officers eventually showed up at my apartment. I told them my concerns, and the history of Katie. The police left for a while — most likely to do some background checks — and then returned. They sat down and one officer looked directly at me. 'We're not prepared to take the children out of here,' he said. Something like that. I couldn't believe it! I was suddenly a single dad raising three children.

Katie showed up at the front door of the apartment building shortly thereafter and the police talked with her. I stood by, watching and listening. She saw Casey walk by inside the building and tried to talk to him, but the police told her not to. They told her to go to court if she wanted to try and get the children back.

I had an excellent lawyer, Andrea, at this time and we went to court right away. For these family court cases, I, on purpose, tried to get a female lawyer, as the system was stacked against men — and a female lawyer questioning your ex-wife was a lot better in court.

I got full custody of all three kids and the money situation reversed also. Katie was supposed to show up on three different occasions, but each time made excuses (at the last second) until the female judge finally had enough of her and awarded me everything. It turned out that it was the same judge who had awarded Katie custody and child support at the beginning. Andrea pointed that out to me.

Back in '95, I had tried to warn the judge that Katie was pawning things off, like the Sega Genesis gaming system

I had bought the kids. But she didn't listen to me the first time around.

For this later case, I did something fun but risky. I dressed in my suit and drove out to a pawn shop in Langford and asked for any information on Katie under a couple of possible aliases.

It's 'possible' they thought I was from a law firm. They gave me a long printout of items she had pawned off. It looked bad on Katie. I presented the details to Andrea, who admonished me for what I had done.

However, I was still glad I had gotten the information. Plus, it was fun to play detective!

# 22

## *Moving*

The one-bedroom apartment on Cook Street was now too small for all four of us. In April, we moved to a two-bedroom townhouse in a run-down white concrete complex, just on the other side of Beacon Hill Park in James Bay. The boys shared a room. Christina had a room. And I had the sofa bed. About twelve families lived there.

To ease the situation for Christina, I decided to get her a cat. We picked out a black one with white spots at the local SPCA. I forget what we named it, but *Hell Cat* would have fit.

The cat never seemed to warm to us and scratched us often. It ran away once or twice, and I regret going out to find it.

I knew nothing about taking care of a cat. But, how hard could it be, right?

The first problem I encountered was the cat litter. The kind I bought was a whitish powdery substance and I got a strange reaction from it.

## CAPE BRETON ORPHAN

One time I was on the phone talking with Ma, standing close to the litter, and it was as if I couldn't think straight. I put the box outside right away.

*Life lesson*: Listen to your body when it's trying to tell you something.

So, I changed the cat litter. The new clumping kind still contained strange chemicals and a strong deodorizer.

I didn't know all that until it was far too late.

One night, while I was trying to sleep downstairs on the sofa bed, my nose kept running and running and running. I went through a lot of tissues. At one point, I suspected that my reaction might be from the cat litter, so I put the container in the backyard.

The next day, we had to drive the cat to the vet for worm treatment. Immediately upon returning, we went out for a walk because I felt nauseated and feared I might collapse. I told the kids to call an ambulance if I fell down. After getting lots of fresh air at the ocean, I felt better.

Back at home, I realized that the cat had tracked litter through the whole place — ever since we got it. I decided to clean everything right away, but using our horrible old vacuum just seemed to put the litter into the air — in smaller particles. *What to do?* I was feeling desperate, so we moved again and got rid of the cat and litter in the process.

However, at the new apartment, I still didn't feel well. One morning, after I took a shower, we all went to see a professional baseball game close by and I had a strange taste on my tongue and felt sick. However, the lights started to go on for me. I wondered about the shampoo and soap. And what about our clothes? What about cat litter and laundry soap? Many questions raced through my mind.

## *Dennis's Wedding*

Around this time, we had been invited to my brother Dennis's wedding in Alberta. My sister asked us to come out early to Saint Paul and said she would take care of us — meaning she would house and feed us for free. Dennis had moved to Saint Paul with his longtime girlfriend, Tara. I made sure that our Unemployment Insurance cheques would be forwarded to Alison's place, bought the kids and me new clothes, and we headed out in our little Hyundai car.

Just a short note on the car: A wonderful lady at my bank had compassion on the kids and me and gave us a small loan to get the secondhand car. When I got layed off, she researched the insurance we had bought (on her advice) and paid off the loan for us. We desperately needed a car at that time. Another example of how one person can make such a difference in the lives of other people.

We caught the ferry and headed for Alberta. The little car drove great and at one point we stopped at a rest place and had a nap. We then continued our journey. Driving in Alberta on the Trans Canada, we passed a large sign that stood in a Farmer's field:

# PREPARE TO MEET THY MAKER

## CAPE BRETON ORPHAN

The kids and I talked about it. A short time later, a big semi-truck pulled out to pass a car and drove straight at us. I could tell immediately that the driver didn't see us and was going to motor right through us. We had nowhere to go and had to pull over quickly to the gravel shoulder. He thundered past, but we were safe! We could have been killed instantly — but God protected us. Maybe the sign had alerted us to the pending danger.

We finally arrived and had a great month or so with Alison, Brian and their two kids, Sarah and Carson. Alison was true to her word and we never paid for anything. They put on great barbeques all the time. However, I still felt somewhat sick at times and was still figuring things out. One day, I went to a doctor in Saint Paul and he informed me about industrial allergies and told me that some people are even allergic to their mattresses.

Back at Alison's, sitting on her deck where we ate and talked often, I realized that her laundry vent came out right there. The exhaust was making me sick. And when I washed the kids clothes in her washer and dryer, I started to think about laundry soap. What kind was she using and how much? I started to think about dryers and things like bounce sheets. I stopped using shampoo, aftershave and underarm deodorant. It would take me months to figure it all out, but everything was making me sick right now. I'm sure that my relatives must have thought I was half-crazy with my photophobia and fragrance intolerance — or whatever it was.

Eventually, the rest of the family made it out from

back east. It was the first time I saw Ma and everyone in about ten years. Ma was her normal self, and was quite overweight. She always struggled with her weight through her adult years. One night while we were all drinking (I think I had one drink that night) and singing around the campfire, Ma was feeling pretty good and made a derogatory remark about Brian's guitar playing and singing. It was embarrassing. We all had to admonish her and stand up for Brian. It was just another example, after all these years, of Ma's behaviour when she drank.

One great thing about getting custody of the children and the sudden health issues, was that I was not drinking or smoking at all. It was so great to be sober all the time. I didn't miss it at all. I had a good buddy in Junior out there, because he had never drank or smoked.

One night, the adults all drove to scout out the hotel and reception room. Ma, Brad and Joy were in one car, and the rest of us were in a van.

Dennis was driving, with Alison also in the front. Junior and I were in the back. For whatever reason, we briefly talked about Ma and our childhood. The question was put out there, 'Would Ma ever apologize for all she had put us through?' There was a general agreement that, no, she would not.

The kids and I had a wonderful time at Alison's before the wedding. The outside wedding was beautiful, but I got another allergy lesson in hair sprays and other strong odours, including the flowers. I couldn't even stay in our hotel room for the reception, spending the night outside in the car. I was also battling all kinds of light situations at the same time. It was crazy.

During my visit, Alison and I had a very interesting talk while relaxing on her back deck one day. She told me that Brian was a highly educated man (he was a counsellor at a First Nations community) and that she and Brian believed that 'God' was just a made-up concept — and that they basically did not believe in him. I guess the kids and I stood out a bit, giving thanks for our meals and such things.

Before I left, I bought Brad and Junior a Bible — as gifts. I also had given one to Dennis and Tara for a wedding present.

I think that my strange health issues and my Christianity (new to them) had my family gossiping. Alison and Dennis never talked to me for about ten years after the wedding. I couldn't figure out why for the longest time. It's not like I was preaching to them, because I wasn't.

### *Back to Victoria*

After the wedding, the kids and I had to get back home. We had to find a new apartment and get ready for school. I had collected a few cheques while out there, but they were not cashed yet. We drove Junior to the airport and said good-bye. The kids and Uncle Junior really got along well.

That was the last time I saw Ma. I saw Junior again in 2009 for the Dragon's Den TV show in Toronto, and I stayed with him when I visited Cape Breton in 2014.

Junior was my closest sibling growing up and it was great to reconnect with him.

My eyes were bad driving back at night time. I was a bit concerned for everyone's safety. Thankfully, we got close behind a big truck and followed his red lights until we got to a hotel.

The following day, we caught the ferry and made it back to Victoria, but now had to look for another place to live. It was getting harder and harder to find a place to rent in Victoria, especially with all the university students looking for a place too.

We first stayed at the Robin Hood hotel on Gorge Street and then another hotel close by. They were renting family suites, so it worked out great for us. I bought some sports toys (for us to play in the parking lot) and dishes and silverware as we had to make our own meals. I found out that we couldn't go on Social Assistance until we used the Unemployment Insurance money we had.

We finally found a place to rent at the Village Green townhouse complex on Menzies Street, in James Bay again, right beside Thrifty's Grocery store. The townhouses were small, two-level wooden structures. A lot of poor and single parents lived in this complex. It was a great location, and only ten minutes away from SJD school on the other side of Beacon Hill Park.

We got settled in our new place and the kids started school. Shortly after we moved in, a nice man brought us some furniture, including some dressers and blankets. He had heard about our plight.

He was a Lutheran man with a Jewish wife and I talked to him a little when he dropped the items off. I had never met him before, but wanted to always remember his kindness.

In about a month, we had spent most of our money. We were getting pretty low on funds and the kids and I prayed together about it. Immediately after we prayed, I had sort of a vision about a cheque in a mailbox. This was not a great, fantastic vision, but was just like when you remember something. I told the kids about it and we decided to go check at the last place we lived. I had no reason to expect a cheque.

Sure enough, the owners of the house told us that there had been mail for us, but they had sent it back. We drove home and phoned Canada Post. They said they could not give us the mail directly, but could deliver it again to the house.

A day or two later, they delivered the mail to the house and we went and picked it up. Among our letters was a government cheque. I opened the envelope in the car: $1,000! It was a rebate of some kind. Regardless of where it had come from or why, we were ecstatic!

I'm so happy that my children got to see these couple of miracles up close while living with me. I hope they'll always remember them. The image of Jesus on the wall and the cheque miracle both happened in a relatively short period of time. We never had anything like that again, although God answers prayers all the time. To me, these were two significant miracles that I never forgot.

# 23

## *The Village Green*

The school year began. Jason was now thirteen-years-old and attended Central School for grade eight. Casey, twelve, entered grade seven at SJD, and Christina, seven, grade two also at SJD. Central was a five-minute walk up the road from Sir James Douglas.

Daily life was a real struggle. I was over-sensitive to everything it seemed. We had to store the mail and papers outside as I couldn't take the smells, inks, and glue.

It was very difficult to do most normal activities, like laundry, showers, and dishes. I couldn't tolerate any cleaning chemicals. A lady I knew recommended household cleaning with vinegar and water.

I found it hard to be in public places, as everyone seemed to be bathed in perfumes, after-shaves and strong laundry smells. Events, like grading from elementary school and Christmas plays, were out for me.

For a time, the kids even did the grocery shopping. Thankfully, the store was right beside us.

## CAPE BRETON ORPHAN

The kids took turns cleaning the bathroom with Sunlight dish soap, as I couldn't use it (just yet). At this time, I washed the dishes with only hot water, and once in a while used a very small amount of soap.

The laundry room vent for the complex was very close to our townhouse. We were bombarded with laundry smells and needed the windows and door closed often. Other smells bothered me too — like diesel and paint fumes. To get from the house to the car, we conducted a big operation each time we left the house.

In the mornings, we would all 'get ready.' Casey would check for smells outside and determine the best route. Then, Jason would open the door. I would walk out fast with my battery-operated mini fan blowing in my face, and march around the corner of the building. Jason would lock the door. The kids would then catch up to me around the building and we'd all walk together to the car.

Sometimes when I drove the children to school, especially in winter, the sun was low and the roads were icy or wet and I would battle bright sunlight reflections. It was hard to handle, so I would wear my oversized sunglasses on top of my normal sunglasses.

My two major health issues made life very hard for the kids, but thankfully, they had school and new friends. I always packed them great lunches. I made big sub buns, with lunch meat, slices of cheddar cheese, and lettuce. We dubbed them Dad's Lunches. I also gave the kids cookies and juice boxes. I felt so great when the boys told me that their friends at school wanted to trade sandwiches.

## The Village Green

When my Unemployment Insurance ran out, and while I battled for Worker's Compensation, we went on Social Assistance. Thankfully, Jason got to join the lunch program at Central, which provided great meals to less fortunate kids. I think we paid a very low amount each month for that. Casey and Christina were able to obtain their musical instruments with a similar program at SJD. Because of those experiences, I'm a strong believer in these programs.

When you go through these hardships of life and get the help that we received through the years, you really want to give back one day. I often think of the poor around us. We currently live close to the Village Green townhouse complex and I often think of the families that live there.

The children also made friends out of the many kids that lived in the Village Green.

Through the next year and a half my days were filled with household chores, reading the Bible and just trying to get healthy.

To accomplish the laundry, I had to gather the clothes and bring them to the laundromat across the street, as the one in our complex had horrible smells inside the old room.

I had to check each washer that I wanted to use to make sure that nothing strong was left over from the previous user. I would wash our clothes with a tiny amount of soap and a lot of water. Sometimes, I needed to put the clothes through again and again with just water — to get smells out.

I hung up the clothes in front of our townhouse on a yellow rope I had strung up. With all our other boxes and papers piled out there, in our very small fenced in yard — I'm sure I looked like a crazy person. There is a great account in the Old Testament about Nebuchadnezzar, the king of Babylon, when he went crazy for some years. His hair and finger nails grew really long and he ate grass like an ox. I felt like I was going mad sometimes. But I knew I wasn't truly crazy because when I was not around these certain soaps and chemicals, I felt fine.

## *Katie and Bill reappear*

In summer 2000, Katie suddenly reappeared. I think the kids told me she was back in town and she dropped by one day. I tried to be graceful as I knew that the kids still loved her deeply, no matter what.

It appeared that her life was getting back together. After talking with her, I helped Katie (and Bill, who was working in the forests far away) to rent a place in the Village Green. They ended up in a townhouse, about thirty feet away, kitty-corner from us.

At first, it was all good. I helped to buy food and Katie cooked meals for the kids (and me sometimes). The kids popped over to see Mom a lot, but I kept a wary eye on her.

Sadly, after a couple of months, she went back to her old habits and it was worse than I thought. She covered her upstairs bedroom window with a blanket, and it looked weird with just a light bulb shining behind it.

## The Village Green

I think spiritually, I just knew that something was off. I think that Katie had slipped into prostitution, as some men, who didn't know who I was, asked me about her.

When Bill was away at his forestry job, Katie started to see different men. Towards the end, there was a new guy staying at her house. I saw him in the doorway once peeking out. He looked like bad news. The Victoria police phoned me one day and told me that he had a gun and they asked me to let them know when he was there. The police did a great job getting rid of him.

Shortly thereafter, Katie abandoned the townhouse. It was hard to believe. The poor kids.

Sometime later, Katie's dad died of cancer. Katie received an inheritance and blew it quickly. She and Bill bought a new truck, rented a place in Sooke (a country area about forty-five minutes away by car), and partied the money away. At one point, the truck got repossessed. Eventually, they rented a place in town, but it all went bad again — so bad that Bill tried to kill himself.

I tried to shield the children as much as I could, but it was extremely difficult. I'm sure the psychological effects of what they had seen and experienced affected them for a long time. Part of Katie's hold on the kids was that she was seen as cool mom — with the parties and music and everything.

She was kind of charismatic that way. She was not really a parent in my opinion, more like a cool friend. I hoped the kids would be able to process all this as they got older.

## CAPE BRETON ORPHAN

Even without my health problems, it would have been tough on the kids moving to a new town, going to a new school, and moving in with a Christian dad. They had gotten used to wild life with Mom, and complete freedom for TV, movies, books, Pokemon cards, and such things.

But I was trying to have a Christian house, and we had to discuss some of these things. I tried to be a good dad and would check the books that they brought home from school (from friends) and talked to them about Pokemon and Yu Gi Oh cards, and soon, Harry Potter. I was also trying to figure these things out for myself.

One of Jason's female friends gave him a book which contained gruesome murders. I explained to him that he should not be reading such things and made him give it back to her. A short time later, I discovered he had the book again. *The joys of parenting.*

During weeknights, we enjoyed listening to a Christian radio show for children: *Adventures in Odyssey.* We loved these shows and got into the great characters and fun story lines. We also played Monopoly and read books, like Dickens, *Treasure Island*, the Hardy Boys and Nancy Drew — plus whatever they brought home from school. I remember Christina bringing home *The Bread Winner.* I enjoyed reading these books with the children.

I taught the boys how to cook French fries in the oven and we ate Hamburger Helper (my speciality at the time). The boys helped with the cooking and chores. However, they had lots of freedom to play with their friends, and had sleepovers at their houses.

## The Village Green

Christina had two close friends, Carly and Sioned, that she met at school, and was soon doing sleepovers at their houses. Casey and Christina sometimes wanted to have their friends over to our house, but in the early years it was near impossible because their friends would have strong shampoo or other smells on them that I couldn't take. I felt bad, but there was nothing I could do. I was very happy that they could go to their friends, as their parents and friends cared about them a lot — and they always had great meals and fun!

Jason and Casey attended Friday night youth nights at a community centre right beside SJD school. Christina and I would drop them off and drive back home. Christina and I then listened to (and sang along with) country music on the radio and she would jump up and down on the bed. Afterwards, we would pick up the boys. Sometimes, if my eyes were not good, Jason would drive the car home. He and the kids really enjoyed that experience!

We also did fun things at the ocean and park. The kids learned to love going down to the ocean during storms. We discovered a great basketball mini court with one basket in the middle of Beacon Hill Park. We played many games there. Casey held the record for the most consecutive baskets for a long time. I think it was fifteen straight from five different spots.

So, there were a lot of good times during the tough years. The roller coaster would continue, but I felt as if I was growing.

# 24

## *The Comeback*

In early 2001, I started jogging very early in the morning, before getting the kids ready for school. I would stop at the top of Beacon Hill Park — in a beautiful spot that overlooks the ocean and huge Olympic Mountains — and pray. I was praying much more in those days and started to feel better. *Was I actually getting better?* I asked my kids if they thought I was improving. They agreed that I was.

One night, as I lay in bed listening to a Vancouver Grizzlies basketball game, an idea for a board game popped into my head. I remember sketching it down. This would become my first game, Crunch Time — a game focused on the fourth quarter of basketball.

The children helped me with colouring in the game board and gave me feedback about what kids like in games. For example, Christina suggested a spinner, and I incorporated that for three-point shots.

I obtained funding from the government for

entrepreneurs on disability, and I was able to hire a graphic artist to do the professional work. We also bought a good second hand van and placed Crunch Time decals on it. I'm sure the kids were embarrassed to drive around in it, but the interior was in great shape and it had tons of room — which would come in handy for the games. It was a huge step up from the Hyundai, which we gave to Katie and Bill.

I now started to see Hayley and Becky more often, and bought Hayley a new bike for her fifth birthday. I also bought the girls a new swing set, but for some strange reason, Lisa rejected it. I realized that Lisa wanted to interfere in my relationship with the girls. I don't think that she was happy that I was on the comeback trail.

At one point, I even tried to reconcile with Lisa, but she rejected me. It was significant for me that I had tried, though, because I think that counted with God. I had been with no one else in all that time. The broken marriage was now on Lisa's account. Not mine.

The girls and I loved to take the van to Peter's Drive-In restaurant close to Beacon Hill park and get an ice cream cone. We would also run around and play at the park. One time, when I returned the girls after a visit, Hayley kept saying that she wanted to spend more time with me. Lisa got very angry at her and threatened to put her in the 'dark room'. I'm sure that Lisa's guard was down when she said that, but I picked it up. It bothered me and I reported it, but later Child and Family Services told me that my concern was unsubstantiated.

# The Comeback

Years later, I got the girls' file from the ministry and found out that they lied to me. What a surprise. Hayley clearly told the worker that they were being locked in a dark room. She said it was pitch black and she thought that there were snakes and bats in the room. The girls used to cry and bang on the door to be let out. It was also revealed that Lisa was spanking them — and that would get much worse in the future.

Jason became more unmanageable in his teenage years. He started to get in trouble at our complex and at school. One night, Jason and the neighbourhood kids had sword fights out in the square between the buildings. Suddenly, the door flew open and there stood the boys – Casey crying and Jason explaining how he hit him in the ear with his stick. Casey's ear was bleeding. I sent Jason upstairs, and followed close behind — very angry. On the stairs, Jason stopped abruptly and I banged into his back with my head. I immediately felt something weird happen in my neck. Jason was as strong as an ox and it was like I hit a brick wall. I gingerly walked downstairs and eventually wrapped a towel around my neck for support. It was a strange injury.

The next day, I had to walk and drive with a towel under my coat for support, as my neck still felt weak. After school, I drove to Central to pick up Jason. He walked up to the car, but didn't get in. He told me, to save our relationship, he was not coming home and was going to stay at a friend's house. I felt very sad and said, 'Don't do this, Jason.' But he had his mind made up.

## CAPE BRETON ORPHAN

My thinking was, you can't force a kid to live with you, and so I accepted his decision. Not that I had much choice.

The good news was that Jason's friend lived close to us and I saw him often. Our relationship would go up and down over the years. Over the next couple of years, he got into more trouble at school and eventually got suspended.

Jason's girlfriend, Zola, and her parents were a great influence on him, though, and when he had to drop out of high school, they were there to help him get into alternative school. In the new school, Jason made me and his mother two incredible silver rings. Mine had three crosses embossed on it and Katie's had a dolphin. I still have mine.

Shortly after that, Zola's mom started to home school Jason and, eventually, helped him to graduate high school.

Somewhere along the line we found out that Katie and Bill had landed in Vancouver.

Close to Christmas, a major bookstore in Victoria, Bolen Books, decided to stock Crunch Time. I had been featured in the local newspaper and TV and sales were good. The book store let me set up a game in the foyer and show it to customers. Casey, Christina and I spent a lot of time in the book store. We loved it as we got to read lots of books and check out other things in the gigantic store. Close to Christmas, the owner, Mel Bolen, handed us a cheque on the way out the door — an early Christmas present!

With Jason gone, any extra chores fell to Casey. He was the one who had to clean the bathroom with the Sunlight soap. Not a fun job. As Casey closed in on fifteen, he was a good kid and we only had a couple of arguments, nothing major. I thought all was well.

One morning in 2002, I woke up and went upstairs to get the children ready for school. Casey was gone, his window open and a letter lying on his dresser. He had jumped down to the covering above the door and made his escape. I found out later that he had stayed at a friend's that night and then left for Vancouver the next day. Casey had gone to live with his mom again. I had underestimated how much they still wanted to be with their mother. When Christina came into the room and found out, she sat down on the bed and cried. I just stood there trying to make sense of it.

Later in the year, Christina and I argued about something and I spanked her (on the bum, fully clothed). I think it was the first and last time I did that. Looking back, it was a mistake. Christina was now ten years old. I then went to the store to buy something and quickly returned. A short time later, Child and Family Services were at my door. Someone had called them.

Outside, in the courtyard, the male worker and I got into a heated argument about spanking. I felt like the Ministry was always on top of me, and this man in particular thought he was saving the world and my children.

The social worker got in my face. I defended myself and told him to back off. Eventually, he left, but the Ministry continued to badger me with phone calls. Over the years they had harassed me with multiple visits, although I never did anything wrong. It's not like they ever offered to help me. It's as if they thought that men just can't be good parents. Their attitude was blatantly sexist. That same attitude ran through other government ministries and family court. I knew it full well.

One day, I asked Christina if she had the choice, would she go and live with her mother. She said, 'Yes'. I therefore agreed that she could, but afterwards wondered if my decision was a mistake.

## *A New Adventure*

In 2003, my health kept improving. I took some general labourer jobs at construction sites, and then landed a job at Thrifty's grocery store in Fairfield — not far from Cook Street. Thrifty's was a large chain of stores on the island, owned by the Campbell family who started them.

The grown children of the owner were the VP's of the company, and I met one of them, Alex Jr. He decided to help me with my game and paid for some travel and hotels, including when I went to Dallas in April, 2004, to sign a Crunch Time deal with NBA star, Dirk Nowitzki – who was from Germany.

In 2004, Nowitzki's agent, Holger, invited me to Germany to meet Nowitzki and promote the game. Holger and his buddy from Nike, Ingo, got me tickets to a big game in Cologne between Team USA and Germany — a tune up game before the Olympics.

## *Rescuing Christina*

Just before I jetted off to Germany in August, I found out that Katie and Bill had a domestic quarrel, and Christina, now twelve years old, had been abandoned at a neighbour's. I quickly made a plan. My older friend, Harvey (a supporter of my new venture) and I, drove over to Vancouver and rescued Christina. I talked to the woman who was watching Christina and asked her some questions. My daughter had truly been abandoned. I still had legal custody of her and had the document with me, so the woman agreed to let me take Christina. We also tracked down Casey and picked him up on the way back to the ferry.

I could tell by Casey's demeanour that he was not keen on coming back to live with me. I don't really know why. I found out later that Katie had recently pawned off some of his electronic toys, including his TV — that he had worked hard for while in Vancouver.

Back in Victoria, Christina stayed at my place for a couple of days, and I got her set up at her friend's house. Sioned's parents were very solid. Her dad was a doctor and her mom was very active at school. I got Casey, who was now seventeen, hooked up with his old friends in Langford and got him a job at Thrifty's — courtesy of Alex, Jr.

The night before I flew out to Germany, there was a knock at my door. I looked out the window and was surprised to see a policeman. He was crouched down on the grass and waved to me.

## CAPE BRETON ORPHAN

I opened the door to my very small bachelor apartment and in flew a gaggle of social workers and cops. They bombarded me with questions about Christina. At that instant, I noticed a red laser dot bouncing around on my chest. I was about to be tasered! I remembered thinking, *don't make any sudden moves.* I was scared. I sat on a chair and just answered their questions.

They had the whole thing wrong, of course, and a phone call to Sioned's parents confirmed that she was in good hands. They also spoke to Carly's mom, who stood up for me too. The police officers and social workers never apologized and seemed confused as they all left my place. Thankfully, I wasn't tasered.

Had someone reported me? I thought so. And for what? Rescuing my daughter? But what can you do? Can you imagine if it was reversed? That a single mom went and rescued her children from a dad who was a known druggie or worse? They would have given her a badge of honour — not threatened to shoot her and remove her children!

I flew out the next day, feeling good that the children were well taken care of.

# 25

## Return to Germany

On my flight to Germany, my seat was close to a washroom, which had a strong soap smell coming from it. The odour increased with each use. I could taste it on my tongue and was getting slightly nauseated. Eventually, I couldn't sit in the area any longer and decided to move towards the front of the aircraft, where the stewardesses were making coffee. I stood against a wall, as there were no empty seats. I was a tiny bit in the way.

Eventually, a head steward, with an attitude, told me to take my seat. I answered him that I could not and suggested he ask some passengers if they could swap seats with me.

At first, he refused to do it and threatened to notify the police when we landed.

I told him that I was travelling to Germany to meet with Dirk Nowitzki and his people. *A great time to drop his name!* This seemed to help and he finally made an announcement.

A passenger volunteered to change seats with me. The steward approached me later, when I was settled and asked me for my name, trying to intimidate me, but I held my ground and told him that I would be reporting *him*. A passenger, who spoke English, supported me at this moment and calmed the situation. When I landed, no police showed up.

This trip was about meeting with Holger, his friend Ingo, and a contact with the German Basketball Federation. It was so great to be back in Germany after all these years. One of the first things I did was have a *Wiener Schnitzel mit Bratkartoffeln* and a beer. And yes, I could enjoy just one beer. I took in a couple of games featuring Team Germany and my contacts invited me to the VIP section before and after each game.

Holger and I made a plan for me to return to Germany in September for the DNBA — The Dirk Nowitzki Basketball Academy — an annual basketball camp for youth in Nowitzki's hometown of Wuerzburg.

## *Meeting Silke*

From 1998 to 2004 I had been single. I dated a woman a couple of times in late 2002, but it didn't work out. In a way, going long periods of time without a woman in my life was like the time I went thirty days without drinking during my Life Skills course in the military. It showed me that I could do it, with God's help.

I returned to Germany and landed in Wuerzburg. The Nowitzki family suggested that I stay at the Gruener

Baum hotel in town. The owners, acquaintances of the Nowitzki's, and their staff were incredibly nice to me. After a few days, they set me up in another hotel, closer to the Nike building where the DNBA was held. My new room was great and was number seven — my favourite number. The art and carpeting were medieval, featuring knights and damsels. The bathroom had a large tub, which I enjoyed during the cool rainy Fall days.

A couple of days later, I met the seven-foot Nowitzki in the gym. It was kind of surreal when Dirk played Crunch Time against me. He kept attempting three-pointer's (with the spinner) and kept missing. He finally cursed. It was not a good sign. However, in the big picture, it was no big deal. Holger and Dirk were very helpful and even allowed me to also produce a figurine of Dirk in the Team Germany uniform, which, I thought would be a great spin-off product.

I decided to develop a website and the German Basketball Federation recommended a freelance graphic artist who worked for them. I met Silke the day before I flew back to Canada. She drove to Wuerzburg and we played Crunch Time on a patio of a fast-food restaurant. It was October 3rd, and unknown to me at the time, it was German Reunification Day.

I returned to Canada and made sure that Christina and Casey were taken care of. I informed Sioned's parents that I would be returning to Germany to market the game. They got me to sign a document to make them guardians while I was away.

My main goal at this point was to make Crunch Time a success and to take care of my children.

Silke and I stayed in contact by email as we planned the website. I needed photos of Nowitzki and lots of data uploaded. As we corresponded, the chatting became more personal. The plan was to produce the game and get it ready for German stores. I returned in early November. Silke helped me as I ran things from Wuerzburg and later from Cologne. She arranged store demonstrations at Kaufhof, a department store chain and translated everything.

Closer to Christmas, Silke and I did a Kaufhof promotion in Munich. We stayed at the former home of Franz Marc, a famous German artist who passed away in the First World War. Silke's family were related to his wife and had inherited the house and some of his pieces. I invented a soccer game, Soccer Tactics (Fussball Taktik) while there.

Germans are crazy about football and we decided to produce this game as Germany would be hosting the 2006 World Cup. The response to Soccer Tactics was excellent and we had our first little hit!

In the summer of 2005, I returned to Canada and attended Casey's high school graduation — even though I couldn't go into the building because of flashes from cameras and strong odours.

I did fly back and forth a few times over the next couple of years, but spent more and more time in Germany, especially during the Christmas season, which is the most important time of the year for selling games.

## Return to Germany

I sent money home for the kids and their caregivers a few times.

Christina had a falling out with Sioned's parents and wanted to live at Carly's house, so I agreed. After some time there, she wanted to stay with a friend from another school, so I allowed that also. Christina was hitting the teen years, and lots of changes were coming.

Back in Germany, I also invented a SciFi game named Ninja Galaxy which was somewhat popular with kids.

We now had three games and were quite busy for the rest of the year, attending game fairs and doing store promos.

In May 2006, I received a phone call from Junior. Ma had passed away. It was weird because I had really wanted to phone her for Mother's Day, but hadn't. We were estranged at this time because I found out that she was corresponding with Lisa behind my back, even though I had asked her not to.

In December, my photophobia flared up again while at a Kaufhof promo. I became sensitive to the bright store lights and my eyes were very weak. Silke had to assist me to the train and take me home. For the rest of my time in Germany, my eyes were very bad and Silke had to take the lead in public.

I tried to return to Canada for Christmas, but couldn't. I had promised Hayley and Becky to attend their Christmas concert, but my eyes were just too bad.

I made two attempts, but couldn't fly out. One time, in Amsterdam, an airline had to remove my luggage from the plane just before take-off, as I couldn't handle the lights and video screens all around me.

In April, Silke accompanied me on the flight to Canada. It was great to be back and I reconnected with the kids. Silke met Hayley and Becky and they really liked her. Silke had to go back soon to Germany, but would return.

I rented an apartment for Christina and me in the Fairfield neighbourhood of Victoria. I was so happy to once again be living close to Cook Street Village, the park and the ocean.

# 26

## *Return to Victoria*

I wanted to make up for lost time. Hayley was almost eleven now, and Becky, almost ten. They asked me to buy them Lululemon hoodies, so we went shopping and they picked their favourite colours. We spent lots of time together at the ocean and Beacon Hill Park, and watched movies at my apartment. Christina, just about fifteen, sometimes joined us for a game of basketball.

By this time, Christina was quite independent. During the school year, I had to push her every morning to get ready for the bus. She would just sit in her room, taking forever to curl her hair and put on make up. She was now into boys and all that. At first, everything worked out well, but eventually Christina wanted to go live with Jason, so I let her.

During one of the visits with the younger girls, Becky innocently told Silke and me about punishment they received at home for not doing their chores properly. She described how they would get spanked by their mother with a spatula 'according to their age'. For example, if you were ten, you got ten whacks, if nine, you got nine. This account set off warning bells for me, because of my knowledge of Lisa's anger and violence, and because these were exceptionally good girls. They were very sweet and polite. We couldn't imagine what they were punished for.

That week, I bought a rubber spatula and smacked my hand with it repeatedly. It really stung and would be equivalent to getting hit with a belt or strap. I found out later that Lisa was following her Brethren church philosophy in disciplining the children, recommended by Dr. James Dobson. I did believe in spanking at the time — but with an open hand on pants. Lisa, however, was hitting them on their bare bums. She also smacked them on their hands for lesser offences, like leaving their shoes out in the hallway and such things.

We found out about another bizarre punishment. Lisa would take away a stuffed toy animal from one of the girls, and put it in a blanket with pockets that hung up somewhere in their house. It was death row for stuffies. That stuffy would hang there for a few days and was on the line. If the child didn't straighten out their act, the stuffy would disappear forever.

I reported Lisa and her 'discipline' to Child and Family Services, but they dropped the ball again. Sexual bias raised its ugly head once more. The social worker told me that the girls just got a spank when they did something wrong, and she never delved deeper into the matter.

Based on that reaction, someone suggested that I

report the discipline to the police. I did, but the female sergeant in charge did not act on it. A couple of weeks later, I complained about her lack of interest in the case. Shortly thereafter, I received a phone call by a police supervisor and he told me that it wasn't right that they had not investigated and they wanted to now. He suggested that I bring the girls in during an access visit, which I did.

The whole situation exploded.

Lisa's aggressive lawyer beat my lawyer to court. They suggested to the court that *I* was harassing Lisa and the girls with my concerns, and therefore *I* should have restrictions placed on *me*. And that's exactly what happened. I could only see the girls in the future with a counsellor or supervisor present. It was beyond frustrating. It was like Orwellian doublethink.

I had originally started court proceedings to get my normal access enforced. Lisa had recently made the children afraid of having overnight visits with me. Lisa went into overdrive with her lying and manipulating and the consequences were devastating.

Now the custody and discipline issues would all be examined by a judge. And unknown to me, this would all take one full year to unfold.

During the court time, it came out that Lisa either lied to or tried to manipulate: teachers, the Ministry of Child and Families, the police, her doctor, a counsellor and the court. She even forged a letter to court, writing as though she was the counsellor. Her own lawyer was shown to be misleading the court by using semantics to lie to the judge. But no matter what I did or what I proved, it didn't matter. The blindfold had slipped off Lady Justice, and the system cared most about the sex of the person in front of them. To think that the Charter of Rights and Freedoms is supposed to protect us from sexual bias. Nope.

And even though Lisa assured the court that she was not alienating the children from me, the strong evidence said otherwise. In the nine years since we attended court, I have not seen the girls once.

How's this for alienation? We found out during the court proceedings that Lisa used to give Becky a quarter so that she would be able to call Lisa or the police in case I tried to kidnap her and her sister.

It was also discovered that Lisa had written a letter to the girls' elementary school — that was kept on file — warning them that I had kidnapped my older children, and that's how I had gotten custody of them. It was hard to believe that any professional would take Lisa or that letter seriously, but because she was a convincing serial liar, they did. And the harm done to the kids and me was great.

To this day, Lisa has never acknowledged her violence, lies and alienation, let alone apologized.

## *Back to Business*

In February 2009, I had another eye incident, this time at the New York Toy Fair. Silke had to host our booth herself. When the exhibition was over, she had to fly out to Germany, and I was left by myself at JFK airport.

*Great*. It was early evening and my flight wasn't until the morning — and the airport was very bright.

I found a small church upstairs, prayed, and tried to sleep on some chairs, but eventually security kicked me out late at night. I managed to survive and, in the morning, Air Canada came to my rescue. The airline switched my flights to get me on an earlier one. Miraculously, the plane was almost empty and I got to stretch out over all the seats in my row and have tea and rest my eyes! It was like heaven. I was so extremely happy to be on that flight and out of NY!

A couple of months later, I was picked to go on the popular TV show Dragon's Den. I wanted to get funding for our somewhat successful board game: Soccer Tactics WORLD. My eyes were extremely sensitive, but I decided to go to Toronto anyway as any publicity would help. CBC didn't contribute any finances for people to come on the show, so I had to spend money we didn't have for the flight and hotel room.

My brother, Junior, arrived the next day. He helped me to get around town and walked me to the show. I had to wear extra pads under my sunglasses as the studio had very bright lights.

The pitch went well, but soon Kevin O'Leary tried to take over with his usual negativity. I got into an epic argument with him. We didn't get the money, but generated tons of publicity when it aired in October.

I was pleased to hear that Robert, one of the dragons, told O'Leary at the end of that show that if O'Leary had talked like that to him, he would have come across the table and hit him. Way to go, Robert!

The episode helped our sales of Soccer Tactics, which would now be stocked by Zellers. We had just got into the department store chain on that trip to Toronto, so I was able to mention it on the show.

The next couple of years were tough because of my eyes and finances. Victoria is a very expensive city and it is hard to find a good place to rent for a reasonable price. However, much to my surprise I started to invent games again, and even started to write.

In 2011, I invented Strikerz Soccer Card Game and in 2012 I wrote a youth book inspired by the game: *The Strikerz*, a story about a bunch of poor soccer phenoms from New Waterford, Cape Breton.

In 2013, I invented a word game called Nuggets. I was inspired by Silke playing an old copy of Scrabble left behind at an apartment we rented. We later changed the name to Wordopolis. Silke and Jason loved playtesting it and so did other word-game lovers.

In 2014, I invented Shooterz Hockey Card Game, which was similar to Strikerz.

In 2014, I also invented Get Adler! Deduction Card Game. Silke worked on the graphics and Mary Yurchesyn, from Cape Breton, drew the cover and character illustrations.

In 2014, we decided to name our little company, Caper Games.

In 2015, I had a heart event.

I had recently felt tired when going for walks. I initially thought it was just a cold, but I felt strange feelings down my arms. When I went to the doctor, he sent me to the hospital right away, but allowed Silke to drive me. I passed all the tests except the treadmill. They drove me a bit hard and the assistant started to get concerned, so they stopped it. They scheduled me for a procedure, at which time they inserted two stents.

I had to have a cloth over my eyes when they performed the procedure, because the overhead light was so bright. However, the whole time I meditated upon Psalm 23, *The Lord is My Shepherd*, and felt totally relaxed through most of it. God really stood with me at that time.

The worst thing that happened during this time, was taking all the drugs afterwards, especially the blood thinners, which sent my heart rate through the roof. Two times within a week or so, I was rushed to emergency. Both times, Silke and I prayed intently and my heart rate returned to normal over hours. The doctor, for the second visit, was surprised when I told him it could come back down to normal, and it did. He had wanted to give me medication for it, but I asked him if we could just wait. God is with us when we need Him the most.

Between 2015 and 2017, off and on, I wrote a novella inspired by Get Adler! *The Adventures of Gold & Sharpe* followed the exploits of MI5 agent Sarah Gold and Inspector Victor Sharpe of Scotland Yard.

In 2017, book selling giant, Barnes & Noble, agreed to stock Get Adler! at over 500 stores across the USA.

That was a big feather in our cap! If we had been bigger, and better able to market and advertise, we could have sold a lot more than the 1,300 copies they ordered, but it was still a great moment and showed us that we could compete with the best companies in the world.

In 2018, I came up with a slogan and an idea for an apparel line. The new slogan was *'cape breton is... my happy place'*. We found a Cape Breton company to embroider the slogan on sweatshirts for us. We were pleased with the result and Capers responded well. We produced a couple of small runs and plan to do more.

In 2018, I invented Vertium: Shadows of the Complex, a SciFi board game for adults and children. We brought it to the market in 2019.

In 2019, we were contacted by a US programmer who wanted to turn our word game, Wordopolis, into a digital game. It is now available for computers and mobile and will soon be on Facebook.

This creative work has given me a lot of satisfaction through the years, and I thank God for every good idea. Silke and I are always so happy to hear when a customer or friend enjoys one of our products.

As I pen the final words of this memoir, I think on what it all means, and I thank you for coming along on my journey.

# 27

## *The End of the Matter*

Sometimes I wonder how my life would have turned out if Alison and I had stayed in Ontario with the Blairs or another good family. Regardless, as I look back over the years with Ma and the various men (father and stepfathers) in my life, I know I have to forgive her. Can I say she did her best under the circumstances? No, I think she could have done a lot better and put her children ahead of herself. But no matter what, I must forgive her and the men for the things I endured that affected my life so greatly.

Those closest to us can do us the greatest harm. I think it's easier to forgive those further away and a lot harder to forgive family and friends — but we have to.

And we must honestly look at ourselves.

My children deserved better from their parents. I could have been a better dad — more loving and patient. I sometimes failed, and I apologize for it. I want my children to know that I pray for them every morning and love them dearly.

I also want my ex-wives to know that I could have been a better husband. I should have been more loving and patient and I apologize for my shortcomings. We have to forgive each other.

Silke and I have been together for fifteen years now. It would be nice to say 'and they lived happily ever after,' but real life is not like that. We have worked very hard on our business and on our marriage, with lots of good days and rough days through the years.

Spiritually, Silke was an atheist when I met her. She became a Christian during our time together, and recently got baptized. We have our own small house church on Sundays, where I read a chapter and we discuss it. We also sing some hymns and praise songs.

We've even been known to sing Christmas carols in the summer. This tradition started one year in Germany, when our car (a high-end Mercedes-Benz that the car rental place gave us as a replacement after a mix-up) broke down on the Autobahn — in Wuerzburg of all places, where we had first met.

After waiting for hours on a scorching hot day, we had the car towed, checked into a local hotel and went for supper. We had a glass of wine with our meal, and — for some unknown reason — sang carols back in our room, laughing non-stop.

Now, every once in a while, we sing carols during non-Christmas times and have a good laugh. We love those Holiday tunes!

# The End of the Matter

## *Spiritual Thoughts*

This book has not been an exhaustive list of all my short-comings or good things that I try to do. I also was argumentative — not just my wives — and also had a short fuse. The good news is that God is still working on me, and that I continue to make progress each year. It's a process.

As a child, teen and young man, I floated through life. The lack of a solid foundation and good parenting really set me back, and I didn't know how to handle important issues.

I was so immature, and still am in some areas — a big kid.

But God is helping me to grow up.

As a new Christian, I should not have gone into ministry so quickly, but God works through our mistakes and weaknesses.

Through all these trials and tribulations, I have become a real person. God has taught me to fight for things. He has made me a fighter.

Through my years in Victoria, I have often had a window that faced the Orion constellation at night time. I always thought of it as *The Fighter* (even though it is officially *The Hunter*), imagining him with a sword and shield.

It has been a great encouragement to me.

I have learned that you have to fight for things in life and in business. No one is going to hand them to you.

My personal goal is to walk more in the Spirit each day.

The Bible tells us that the fruit (evidence or outworking of the Holy Spirit) is: *love, joy, peace, patience, kindness, goodness, gentleness, faith and self-control.* I think we can all use a bit more of those characteristics in our lives. I know I can.

## *What is Success?*

After many years of working on the games, I sometimes thought, *what if I fail?* What if, after all this running, the business didn't work out? And yet, I have never dwelt long on those doubts. God has given me faith in Him and faith in what I'm doing. If the business doesn't pan out in the end, it has nothing to do with the truth of God. My eternal destiny is not dependent upon the success of the products and company.

Success in the business world for me would mean that I could help the poor and needy a lot more, and take better care of my family.

I think of Cape Breton often. I would love to be successful and help create employment so Capers could stay home and not have to move away for work.

I believe that God has been faithful to my prayers and efforts through these many years, even though it's been tough.

It was a great moment for our little company in 2017, when the buyer for bookstore giant Barnes & Noble loved our new game, Get Adler! and stocked it.

## Spiritual Success

*I will not leave you as orphans: I will come to you.*
John, chapter 14.

When God saves you, he adopts you into his family. He becomes your Father — the best one you will ever have. You will never be alone again. He will never leave you nor forsake you.

Many people have had the same life experience as I: feeling lonely or empty, and filling that void with alcohol, drugs, sex, relationships, entertainment or whatever. And many Christians have testified, that after they got saved, that void was filled.

That is how I feel. God has filled the void.

I have made some major mistakes in my life and committed some major sins — but not on purpose. I made mistakes because of ignorance or weakness or stupidity. However, the good news is that God's love and grace are greater than all my sins (and yours).

I have not smoked in over 21 years. I almost never drink, and when I do, it is only one or two beers or a glass of wine. God has completely taken alcoholism out of my life. I never go to bars or dancing clubs (not that I'm against dancing).

I have been with only one woman for the past twenty years. For me, this is a major accomplishment.

There was a time when I could not get a girlfriend, let alone a wife.

Then there came a time when I had too many women in my life.

I think the dream in Sardinia, Italy, about the many women, may have been a tip-off for what was to come. Could it be that God had compassion on a lost and lonely orphan?

I am certainly not perfect, and some days far from it, but I can look back and see the work of God in my life — and know he has my today and my future.

In conclusion, there is spiritual success and physical success, but the things of this world are not going to last. So we must focus on our walk with God, and use our gifts in this life to bless others. God is good. He is gracious.

*I will not leave you as orphans ....*

Thank you, Lord.

# *Acknowledgements*

I would like to thank Silke for her editing, graphic artwork, typesetting, and for pushing me to write better. She did a wonderful job while struggling with her own eye issues.

I would like to thank Jill Corley for proofreading the final manuscript and for her excellent suggestions.

I would like to thank the members of our Cape Breton Orphan Facebook group, who read the early chapters, picked up errors, and encouraged me often. I want to especially thank:

Judy Urquhart
Sharon Randles
Damien Scott
Sylvia Melanson
Nora Campbell
Martin Malik
Michelle Bates

Randall James Thompson
is a game designer and author with Caper Games.

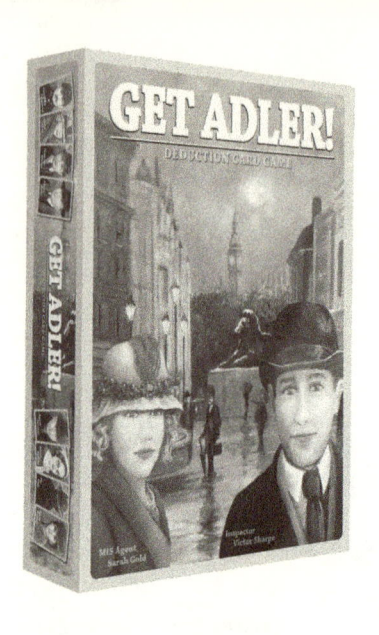

# Get Adler!
## DEDUCTION CARD GAME

London, 1937 — Intelligence has discovered that Top-Secret documents are missing. So, too, is MI6 Agent Adler! The only clue is an intercepted message: 'Trafalgar at seven'. MI5 Agent Gold, Inspector Sharpe of Scotland Yard, and Constable Townsend have been thrown this task: Find and eliminate Adler! They've got seven hours.

Get Adler! is a multi-player card game in which secret characters investigate each other to unmask Adler. Once the traitor is revealed, the game transforms into an action-packed race against time to eliminate Adler and to recover Top-Secret documents.

**Time: 30 min. / Ages: 9+ / Players: 4 - 8**

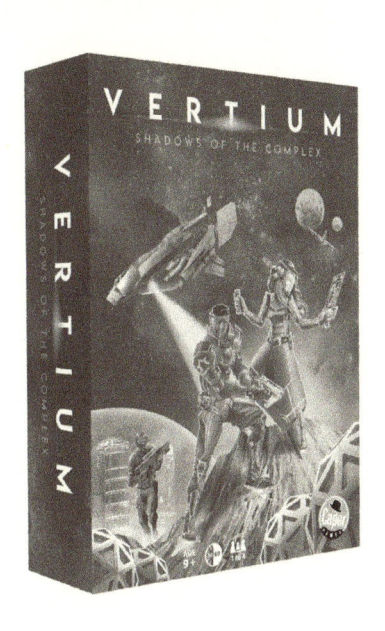

# Vertium
## SCI-Fi BOARD GAME

Vertium is a quick and tactical space colonization game for 1 to 4 players. Players are faction Commanders directing their Captains to claim planets and mine the powerful radioactive element Vertium.

As influential moons orbit the colonized planets, additional Vertium is gained. However, you'll have to be wise and courageous because your rivals have their eyes on your spheres and resources. Prepare for conflict.

**Time: 30-60 min. / Ages: 9+ / Players: 1 - 4**

# www.capergames.ca

CPSIA information can be obtained
at www.ICGtesting.com
Printed in the USA
LVHW091600051221
705334LV00004B/123

9 781714 489534